Testing
the Global Ethic

Voices from Religious Traditions on
Moral Values

Edited by
Peggy Morgan
and
Marcus Braybrooke

International Interfaith Centre,
and
The World Congress of Faiths
2 Market Street, Oxford OX1 3EF, UK

CoNexus Press,
6264 Grand River Drive, Ada, MI 49301, USA

First published 1998

There will be no human life together without a
world ethic for the nations

There will be no peace among the nations without
peace among the religions

There will be no peace among the religions without
dialogue among the religions

(Hans Küng, *Global Responsibility*, p.138)

International Interfaith Centre and
The World Congress of Faiths
2 Market Street,
Oxford OX1 3EF, UK
ISBN 0 95 24140 1 5
Tel: 44(0) 1865 202745 Fax 44(0) 1865 202746
e-mail: iic@interfaith-center.org.

CoNexus Press,
6264 Grand River Drive,
Ada, MI 49301, USA
ISBN 0 9637897 6 7
Tel: 616 682 9022 Fax 616 682 9023
e-mail:conexus@iserv.net.

CONTENTS

ACKNOWLEDGMENTS

Pictures

Thanks are expressed to the Council for a Parliament of the World's Religions, PO Box 1630, Chicago, IL 60690–1630, USA for the picture of the 1993 Assembly by John Reilly; to the British Museum for the Babylonian Map of the World; to Archbishop Damianos and the monks of St Catherine's Monastery, Sinai for permission to reproduce the picture of Christ Pantocrator; to the World Council of Churches for the Japanese picture of Jesus; to Dejazumah Johnson of R.U.Z. for the picture of Emperor Haile Selassie I and for the Lion of Judah, to United Press International for the picture of Martin Luther King from *My Life With Martin Luther King Jr* by Coretta Scott King, published by Holt, Rinehart and Winston, Inc, New York and Hodder and Stoughton, London 1969; to Ann and Bury Peerless for the picture of the Jain monk; to Mark Simmons for the picture of Sukkot; to Wendy Adams at USPG and to the United Society for the Propogation of the Gospel for picture of a baptism; to Mrs Riadh El Droubie for use of her late husband's picture of Muslims at prayer; to the Kupferstich-Kabinett, Staatliche Kunstsammlungen, Dresden for the picture of Immanuel Kant and to contributors for other pictures.

Contributors

Charanjit Ajitsingh

Mavis Badawi

Martine Batchelor

Shahin Bekhradnia

Andrew Bolton

Bronwyn Elsmore

S L Gandhi

Arthur Dion Hanna, jr

Clive Lawton

Sister Maureen Goodman

Werner Menski

Rachel Montagu

John Newsom

Glynn S Phillips

Editors

Peggy Morgan

Marcus Braybrooke

PREFACE

'Time to make a difference' is the overall theme of the Millennium Exhibition to be held in London. During extensive consultation the planners of the exhibition found that the great majority of people wanted the Millennium 'to make the world a better place'. A similar hope is to be found in many of the religious traditions, although their suggestions about how such an improvement is to be achieved vary considerably. Even so, is there enough agreement in the teaching of the religions for their members to have a common message to the world at the start of a new millennium?

This is the claim of those who endorsed *A Declaration Toward a Global Ethic* at the 1993 Parliament of the World's Religions. Can such a claim be justified from the teaching of the religions? This is the question we asked the contributors to this book. We began with two daylong consultations to get to know each other, to discuss the *Global Ethic* and to agree on our approach. Some contributors had serious questions about the methodology of the *Global Ethic* and whether it was too western. Does the very concept of the global suggest a denial of the particular? Can a religion's ethical teaching be separated from the wider framework of beliefs and practices?

Despite some hesitations, the contributors accepted working within the framework of the *Global Ethic* and agreed to say what their religion taught about 'being fully human' and about the directives, as well as about 'the transformation of life'. Originally we were going to call the book 'Trialing the Global Ethic', as you the readers are the jury to judge whether there is enough agreement to support the claim that the religions have a common message, but there was no agreement on whether one can use the word 'trial' as a verb!

If a *Global Ethic* is indeed to command world-wide support it will need to be authenticated in a very large number of religious traditions. Although not all faiths could be represented nor all express their views on every issue, contributors include a Zoroastrian, a Baha'i and a Rastafarian, as well as members of the six so-called 'world religions'. There is also a contribution from someone with a non-religious viewpoint and a member of a new spiritual movement. We have in several cases involved two people from a religious tradition to emphasise that no religious tradition is monolithic. We hope the book enshrines the principle of dialogue and encourages you to reflect on how the ethical principles which guide your life relate to the *Global Ethic*.

The importance of the *Global Ethic* and therefore of this book is that as 'the global city' becomes ever more plural and interdependent, we need to find shared values for our common life. As Hans Küng has said 'there will be no human life together without a world ethic for the nations'.[1]

The book, therefore, is relevant to all who are concerned with the future of our societies and our world. It is especially relevant for the young, so we hope it will be a resource book for teachers in a number of areas, including education in personal, social and moral values, citizenship and religions, not only in Britain and North America, but across the world.

The book is an original contribution to the discussion about a global ethic and shared values in a plural society, but it could also be used for information about the teachings of particular religions (e.g. what do Sikhs say about war and peace?). The book also provides resources for discussion in interfaith groups and indeed amongst members of one faith who wish to see how their teachings relate to the teachings of others.

It is hoped that this book will be a useful resource in a wide variety of educational situations. Teachers will be able to add their own examples to what we have begun. Students will also be able to make their own contributions in each area on the basis of the stimulus given. The text is intended to be open to growth in that way and is not seen as definitive, either in the case of the individual religions or the variety of worldviews generally. It begins the further discussion that is needed across the world about these important issues and in that discussion adds stimulus to co-operation and action. As we want the book to be widely used, permission is given to teachers and religious educators, with due acknowledgement, to photocopy material from the book for use in group discussion.

We are very grateful to all the contributors for their willing participation. We also wish to thank Professor Hans Küng and the Global Ethic Foundation, and Sir Sigmund Sternberg, Founder of the Three Faiths Forum, for their encouragement and financial support with this project. We also express our gratitude to Celia Storey and Sandy Martin, the Co-ordinators of the International Interfaith Centre and hope this project will be a significant contribution to the Centre's research programme. We also express our thanks to Diana Hanmer, Office Secretary of the World Congress of Faiths, to all the staff of Quorn Litho, to Joel Beversluis of CoNexus Press for their help, to Jim Kenney of the Council for a Parliament of the World's Religions for reading the text, to Brian Pearce of the Inter Faith Network for his advice and to those who supplied pictures. Very particularly, we wish to record our deep appreciation of Sally Richmond's care and patience in the preparation of the material for the printer. She was assisted with the page lay-out by Richard Westgarth. Our thanks also to the Central Board of Finance of the Church of England, for permission to quote from the Alternative Marriage Service.

Peggy Morgan

Marcus Braybrooke

August 1998

SECTION A

Introduction

Ancient Guidelines:

The Golden Rule

Baha'i

Blessed is he who preferreth his brother before himself.

Tablets of Bah'a'ullah, 71.

Buddhism

A state which is not pleasant or enjoyable for me will not be so for another; and how can I impose on another a state which is not pleasant or enjoyable for me?

Samyutta Nikaya, V.

ConfucianIsm

Do not do to others what you do not want them to do to you.

Analects 15, 23.

Christianity

All things whatsoever ye would that others should do to you, do ye even so to them.

Matthew 7, 12.

Hinduism

This is the sum of duty; do naught unto others which would cause you pain if done to you.

Mahabharata, XIII, 114.

Islam

No one of you is a believer until he desires for his brother that which he desires for himself.

An-Nawawi, 40 Hadith, 13.

Jainism

A person should treat all creatures as he himself would be treated.

Sutrakritanga 1.11.33.

WHAT IS THE GLOBAL ETHIC?

At the 1993 Parliament of the World's Religions at Chicago in 1993. most members of the Assembly of Spiritual Leaders endorsed the Global Ethic. ©*John Reilly.*

Is there anything on which all religions can agree? The Global Ethic claims that: *'There is a principle which is found and has persisted in many religions and ethical traditions of humankind for thousands of years: What you do not wish done to yourself, do not do to others! Or in positive terms: What you wish done to yourself, do to others!'* Or as the Global Ethic itself puts it: *'We must treat others as we wish others to treat us'.*

This claim may seem surprising as history is full of wars about religion, such as the Crusades. Even today religious differences have made conflicts in Northern Ireland or the Middle East more bitter. The claim may also seem surprising as religions disagree about their ideas concerning ultimate reality and how people should live their lives.

Parliaments of World Religions.

Just over one hundred years ago, a first attempt was made to bring together representatives of all religions to a World Parliament of Religions. This was held at Chicago in 1893 as part of the World Fair, which marked the four hundredth anniversary of the 'discovery' of America by Christopher Columbus. Charles Bonney, an American lawyer, whose idea it was to hold the Parliament, hoped *'to unite all religion against all irreligion and to make the Golden Rule the basis of this union.'*

In 1993, another Parliament of the World's Religions was again held in Chicago. In the century between the two Parliaments, a lot has been done to encourage people of different religions to learn about each other's beliefs and to get to know each other. This is often called 'interfaith dialogue'. Now, there is an even more urgent desire for people of all religions to act together to help a suffering world. At the 1993

Judaism

You shall love your neighbour as yourself.

Leviticus 19, 18.

Native American

Respect for life is the foundation.

The Great Law of Peace

Sikhism

Do not create enmity with anyone as God is within everyone.

Guru Arjan Devji 258, Guru Granth Sahib

Zoroastrianism

That nature only is good when it shall not do unto another whatever is not good for its own self.

Dadistan-i-Dinik, 94,5.

Parliament leading members of many religions signed the Declaration Toward a Global Ethic.

Declaration Towards A Global Ethic.

As a result of much meeting and talking, many members of all religions recognise that despite important differences of beliefs and practices, there is basic agreement on moral and ethical principles. They also believe that it is vital for this agreement to be better known so as to inspire people of all faiths together to tackle the great problems of war and violence, of poverty and hunger and of threats to the environment, because as the Declaration says, *'the world is in agony...peace eludes us... the planet is being destroyed... neighbours live in fear... women and men are estranged from each other ... children die'.*

The basic ethical principle is *'that every human being must be treated humanely. This means that every human being without distinction of age, sex, race, skin, colour, physical or mental ability, language, religion, political view, or national or social origin possesses an inalienable and untouchable dignity'.*

Four Directives.

If everybody is to be treated as having an inherent right to a fully human life, then, the Declaration says, there are four guidelines or irrevocable directives for behaviour;

1. Commitment to a culture of non-violence and respect for life.

This would mean banning war, unfair imprisonment, torture and perhaps making the arms trade unnecessary, as well as protecting animals and plants.

2. Commitment to a culture of solidarity and a just economic order.

This would ensure a basic standard of living for all people, do away with exploitation, such as child labour and require a fair system of international trade, which might mean cancelling Third World debts and checking the power of multi-national companies.

3. Commitment to a culture of tolerance and a life of truthfulness.

This would mean that politicians always told the truth, that nations honoured the treaties which they signed and that the media were fair and unbiased.

4. Commitment to a culture of equal rights and partnership between men and women.

Religions have often not practised this themselves, but changes are taking place as women begin to take positions of leader-

3

The Symbol of the Council for a Parliament of the World's Religions.

ship in some religious traditions. Many religious people are campaigning against child pornography and against the international sex trade.

Attempts are now being made to see how adherence to these four irrevocable directives should be applied in key areas of our life together. In preparation for the next Parliament of the World's Religions, which is to be held in South Africa in 1999, a Call to the Guiding Institutions is to be issued. This would indicate how the irrevocable directives might be applied, for example, in economic and political life.

Questions

Not everyone is persuaded that religions do agree on basic ethical principles. Even at the 1993 Parliament there was disagreement about 'non-violence'. Does this rule out the right to self-defence? Would it prevent the United Nations sending a 'peace-keeping' force to a troubled area of the world? Others thought that the Declaration said too little about the environment. Others questioned whether there are universal moral values. Some people suggested that the declaration was an attempt to impose 'Western' values on the rest of the world. Other people do not think that moral teaching can be separated from the beliefs of a particular religion of which that moral teaching is a part.

The Global Ethic needs to be tested to see whether it does indeed represent the teachings and practices of people of many religions. In this book, people of different religions discuss what they think being 'fully human' means and whether their religious teachings support the four 'irrevocable directives'.

Those who signed the *Declaration Toward A Global Ethic* at Chicago in 1993 said: '*We commit ourselves to this global ethic, to understanding one another, and to socially-beneficial, peace-fostering, and nature-friendly ways of life. We invite all people, whether religious or not, to do the same*'.

How would you respond to that invitation?

Think of one socially beneficial teaching you would support and of one socially beneficial action, one peace-fostering action, one nature-friendly action that you would support. Reading what members of different religions think may help you to make up your mind and will be one step towards a better understanding of each other.

The 1993 Declaration Toward a Global Ethic

The world is in agony. The agony is so pervasive and urgent that we are compelled to name its manifestations so that the depth of this pain may be made clear.

Peace eludes us . . . the planet is being destroyed . . . neighbours live in fear . . . women and men are estranged from each other . . . children die.

This is abhorrent!

We condemn the abuses of earth's ecosystems.

We condemn the poverty that stifles life's potential; the hunger that weakens the human body; the economic disparities that threaten so many families with ruin.

We condemn the social disarray of the nations; the disregard for justice which pushes citizens to the margin; the anarchy overtaking our communities; and the insane death of children from violence. In particular we condemn aggression and hatreds in the name of religion.

But this agony need not be.

It need not be because the basis for an ethic already exists. This ethic offers the possibility of a better individual and global order, and leads individuals away from despair and societies away from chaos.

We are women and men who have embraced the precepts and practices of the world's religions.

We affirm that a common set of core values is found in the teachings of the religions, and that these form the basis of a global ethic.

We affirm that this truth is already known, but yet to be believed in heart and action.

We affirm that there is an irrevocable, unconditional norm for all areas of life, for families and communities, for races, nations and religions. There already exist ancient guidelines for human behaviour which are found in the teachings of the religions of the world and which are the conditions for a sustainable world order.

We declare:

We are interdependent. Each of us depends on the well-being of the whole, and so we have respect for the community of living beings, for people, animals, and plants, and for the preservation of Earth, the air, water and soil.

We take individual responsibility for all we do. All our decisions, actions, and failures to act have consequences.

We must treat others as we wish others to treat us. We make a commitment to respect life and dignity, individuality and diversity, so that every person is treated humanely, without exception. We must have patience and acceptance. We must be able to forgive, learning from the past but never allowing ourselves to be enslaved by memories of hate. Opening our hearts to one another, we must sink our narrow differences for the cause of world community, practising a culture of solidarity and relatedness.

We consider humankind our family. We must strive to be kind and generous. We must not live for ourselves alone, but should also serve others, never forgetting the children, the aged, the poor, the suffering, the disabled, the refugees, and the lonely. No person should ever be considered or treated as a second-class citizen, or be exploited in any way whatsoever. There should be equal partnership between men and women. We must not commit any kind of sexual immorality. We must put behind us all forms of domination or abuse.

We commit ourselves to a culture of non-violence, respect, justice and peace. We shall not oppress, injure torture, or kill other human beings, forsaking violence as a means of settling differences.

We must strive for a just social and economic order, in which everyone has an equal chance to reach full potential as a human being. We must speak and act truthfully and with compassion, dealing fairly with all, and avoiding prejudice and hatred. We must not steal. We must move beyond the dominance of greed for power, prestige, money, and consumption to make a just and peaceful world. Earth cannot be changed for the better unless the consciousness of individuals is changed first. We pledge to increase our awareness by disciplining our minds, by meditation, by prayer, or by positive thinking. Without risk and a readiness to sacrifice there can be no fundamental change in our situation. Therefore we commit ourselves to this global ethic, to understanding one another, and to socially-beneficial, peace-fostering, and nature-friendly ways of life.

We invite all people, whether religious or not, to do the same.

The Declaration Toward a Global Ethic is printed as the Introduction to *A Global Ethic*, Ed. Hans Küng and Karl-Josef Kuschel, SCM Press and Continuum 1993, which contains the fuller text and explanation prepared by Professor Hans Küng.

This Babylonian clay tablet preserves a representation of the world dating from the fifth century BCE. ©The British Museum.

QUESTIONING AND TESTING THE GLOBAL ETHIC

WHY A TRIAL IS NEEDED

I am going to start my discussion of issues relating to the global ethic, which is intended to be an interactive discussion with you, the reader, by referring to the statement that 'the world is in agony'.

First of all, think about this language of 'world'. Have you ever looked at old maps and been surprised at how people have seen 'the world' at different times? Sometimes whole areas that we now hear about every day were not known. Sometimes continents are a completely different shape. Japanese and Chinese maps present the world quite differently from European maps; tenth century maps vary enormously from those of the twentieth century.

Think about the emergence of the current language of 'global' and 'one world' with our image of a single planet. It seems to derive from the images sent back by the 1969 Apollo space mission and seeing the whole earth and earthrise from space. Since then thinking globally has become very fashionable, but can lead people to ignore the local and the positive things about diversity and difference. Added to that are issues like the concern to provide tomatoes on supermarket shelves everywhere all the year round which can lead to the decline of the local market gardener, local varieties and market stalls. Who has decided which kind of tomato is to be grown? If you transfer that kind of query to a concept like that of equality it is a good basis for criticising high-flown, sweeping statements which assume that everyone has accepted or is assumed to have, the same idea of equality.

Whatever your age, put down, **in one word**, how you think the world is getting on. Can you select (or create) a picture or a story of how the world is for you? Your example might be a great work of art or literature or an advertising image. From your knowledge of history can you think of how a person from a different century and place might have answered this question? Examples might be an Indian village woman in the eleventh century, someone in Spain at the time of the inquisition, a Chinese farmer in the fourteenth century, an English landowner in the seventeenth century, an American soldier at the time of the civil war. Also ask yourself and discuss with others whether we should talk about individual agonies or local agonies rather than 'world' agony. How do these differ from and how affect each other? Is the agony of the 'world' different from the sum total of the other agonies and if so how is it different? Is it just that we are more aware of the sum total of agony because of mass communications? But if all the local agonies were healed, all would be well.

Would I be asking you the same question if I asked how the planet is getting on? Is planet a term which is more inclusive of other than human living beings, such as trees and animals, with which we share this planet? Is using planet, like using the term Gaia, rather than globe, an ethical shift of language that indicates that we need to be sensitive to the elephants' and oaks' experience of the world as much as the views of other human beings? And if you respond that these are not views we can know, then I would suggest that imagination and rational discussion can provide this picture just as clearly as for any of the humans about and for whom we assume we can speak. How far do religions take account of the variety of all living things and beings on the planet? How far does the global ethic as it stands take account of them or is it too human-centred?

Just as old maps are entirely the product of one explorer or civilisation's view of the world as they knew it, so the popular language of 'global' is a product of our age's discoveries and perspectives. Be aware in all that you read and hear how often the language of 'global' and 'world' occurs. Using it is very much the fashion of the age and might, in reference to politics and economics be rather imperialistic!

The teachings of religious traditions may say that they bring to the question of the state of the world key teachings that focus on the inadequacies of life at any time compared with how things should be and ultimately are. This sense is inherent in the Indian term samsara and in the Christian teaching that the world is fallen and a vale of tears. They also have a vision of how things should be and the paths to those ideals. Ethics are part of the whole framework of understanding in these traditions and cannot be separated from the other dimensions of religions such as doctrines, communities, narratives, rituals and experiences. An emphasis on ethics isolated from these other dimensions may derive too strongly from the eighteenth century philosopher Kant and the European Enlightenment to be particularly sympathetic to members of all religious traditions, even though all have ethical teachings.

Another key question for those who articulate a global ethic is whether it is **words** that effect ethical change in people's lives. Would it not be helpful if documents were combined with tangible programmes of joint action? Will asserting what we 'must' do help people to change? If, as it is asserted, common teachings are already present in all the key traditions, then why is the world not transformed where members of those traditions are dominant? It has been pointed out that religions have often contributed to injustice, intolerance and violence. The key question then is **how** lives are changed. This is the substance of the last section on the transformation of life. Is there any agreement on the **how**, and have the suggested practices of the traditions been successful? The answer is likely to be 'sometimes **yes** and sometimes **no**'. What also, as our philosopher asks, are the other factors contributing to the agony of the world and how can they be faced and overcome by everyone, whether religious or not?

Some of our contributors are critical of what they see as the Christian style of the language of the original declaration, pointing out that *their* traditions have important ethical principles but that they are not expressed in the same way and that the paradigms and inter-relationships vary. For example equality is often discussed in matters of ethics, but it is not a term that everyone likes. Some, like our Muslim contributor, prefer to talk about equity and Buddhists and Hindus like to emphasise interconnectedness. We then have to ask about equality of voices. Where are the children's voices in religious traditions? Trees (as well as babies and mentally or physically challenged human beings) cannot speak. Does that mean they do not matter? Can there be equality when language is not gender-sensitive? Why are most of the world's religious leaders men and what do ordinary people say? Religious people **within** traditions often disagree with each other, so can there ever really be full agreement across traditions? One example emerged in the planning of this book. As an earlier chapter points out, we wanted to include more than one voice within traditions where possible. But one person, having accepted our invitation to join the writing group, found out that there was to be another person from a different sectarian group in his tradition making a contribution and so, instead of being prepared to discuss and articulate differences in the final text, withdrew. To acknowledge the potential for diversity within traditions, we have called each section 'a view on' though some writers have written in terms of what they think 'the tradition' says and are prepared to be more sweeping than others.

At all times the reader needs to carry these questions and others that they have to the text and from that into creative dialogue, and perhaps action, with those from religious traditions and worldviews other than their own. We have begun the process of testing, its continuation lies with you, the reader.

SECTION B

What does it mean to be fully human?

The basic ethical principle suggests *'that every human being must be treated humanely. This means that every human being without distinction of age, sex, race, skin colour, physical or mental ability, language, religion, political view; or national or social origin possesses an inalienable and untouchable dignity'.*

A BAHA'I VIEW OF WHAT IT MEANS TO BE FULLY HUMAN

True life is not the life of the flesh but the life of the spirit.

Baha'u'llah, *Kitab-i-Iqan: The Book of Certitude* 77-78

The rewards of the other world are the perfections and the peace obtained in the spiritual worlds after leaving this world, while the rewards of this life are the real luminous perfections which are realized in this world, and which are the cause of eternal life, for they are the very progress of existence.

'Abdu'l-Baha, *Some Answered Questions* 224

Progress and barbarism go hand in hand, unless material civilization be confirmed by Divine Guidance, by the revelations of the All-Merciful and by godly virtues, and be reinforced by spiritual conduct, by the ideals of the Kingdom and by the outpourings of the Realm of Might.

Selections from the Writings of 'Abdu'l-Baha 284

We must strive unceasingly and without rest to accomplish the development of the spiritual nature in man, and endeavour with tireless energy to advance humanity toward the nobility of its true and intended station.

'Abdu'l-Baha, *Baha'i World Faith* 262

It is religion ... which produces all human virtues, and it is these virtues which are the bright candles of civilization.

'Abdu'l-Baha *Secret of Divine Civilization* 98

Most religions say this world is not an ideal place and tell us that rather than concentrate on worldly things, we should set our sights on spiritual values – the spiritual life to come after our physical death is said to be our real goal.

Then what is the purpose of this earthly existence? Why do we have this physical life at all – why not skip it all together and have just the spiritual life to come?

The Baha'i Writings say the reason we are here is to learn and gain virtues – a physical existence helps us to learn lessons.

In our human life, following a time as a developing foetus, we are born as a baby with no knowledge of the world. As we progress through the stages of infancy, childhood, youth, maturity, and old age, we learn through experience. For instance, if there was no such thing as childhood and youth, we would not understand the notion of maturity; just as we grasp the idea of health because we see examples of sickness.

In the various levels of existence in this world – the mineral, vegetable, and animal kingdoms – humans recognize themselves as making up the top level of the highest kingdom, but we can still improve further. People have extra gifts of reasoning, being able to use abstract thought, creativity and invention – attributes which should lead us to ever higher attainment.

Our experience does not end with our physical death. The human 'soul' continues to exist in a 'spiritual' state. But unless we work in this life to gain virtues and perfections, we will be handicapped in the spiritual world, as we lack the qualities to progress further. In this existence we should develop spiritual qualities which help to perfect our characters.

In each person's life there should be evolution upward – we improve ourselves by acquiring virtues such as honesty, love, justice, kindness.

Just as each person should gain spiritual qualities, there is also a collective goal – the day by day, age by age, attainment of a higher degree of civilization on earth.

The unideal state of the world comes about because most people do not understand the purpose of life, and act in ways contrary to our happiness. This can change by individuals acquiring human virtues which are the

The Divine religions, the holy precepts, the heavenly teachings, are the unassailable basis of human happiness ... the peoples of the world can hope for no real relief or deliverance without this one great remedy.

'Abdu'l-Baha, *Secret of Divine Civilization* 99

Strive with heart and soul in order that day by day the world of humanity may become more glorious, more spiritual, more sanctified; and that the splendour of the Sun of Reality may be revealed fully in human hearts as in a mirror. This is worthy of the world of mankind. This is the true evolution and progress of humanity.

'Abdu'l-Baha, *Baha'i World Faith* 262

Briefly; the journey of the soul is necessary. The pathway of life is the road which leads to divine knowledge and attainment. Without training and guidance the soul could never progress beyond the conditions of its lower nature which is ignorant and defective.

'Abdu'l-Baha, *Foundations of World Unity* 78

'bright candles of civilization'. With the lighting of enough 'bright candles' of love and peace the world will be flooded with light. Some religions refer to this improved state as the Kingdom of God.

The importance of this world is its value to teach us, individually and collectively, how we can raise ourselves to a higher state. The physical world clearly shows how each action has a reaction – physical senses such as sight, hearing and others let us see what actions have good or bad results – and the lessons we learn here help guide us in our progress in our spiritual lives. Humankind collectively should also see what works to advance civilization and elevate the world of humanity.

Over centuries and ages the standard of civilization has been raised. This is seen easily in the area of material improvements, but unless physical advances are balanced with spiritual perfections, there is a danger that knowledge can work against continuing progress. True advancement can continue only through the efforts of each component member.

As civilization increases, individual progress will become easier to achieve as spiritual qualities will be more widespread; but since the perfection of individuals is needed to raise the standard of our world, the two processes must proceed together.

People should not live lives of austerity and asceticism. The things of the earth are here for us to use and enjoy – but in moderation and within the limits that one does no harm to others. By living our life we gain experiences and learn.

Questions

What are the lessons, from a Baha'i viewpoint that we should learn from our physical existence:

(a) individually ?

(b) collectively ?

Do you agree that over centuries the standard of civilization has been raised ?

No one can see the soul. The soul sees the body. The body cannot see the soul. When the soul leaves, the body becomes inert. The soul cannot be seen, the body can be seen.

(*The Murli*, teachings given through Brahma Baba, the Founder of the Spiritual University)

When spiritual love prevails, neither internal nor external animosity, hatred, anger or jealousy are possible. Negative feelings are transformed into positive feelings with the coolness of love. In spiritual love there is harmony, since love removes controlling or co-dependent tendencies and ensures kindness, caring and amicable understanding.

(*Living Values* : A Guidebook published by the Brahma Kumaris)

Think of a situation of conflict in your own life. Can you change that situation by being loving?

Peace consists of pure thoughts, pure feelings, and pure wishes. When the energy of thought, word, and action is balanced, stable and non-violent, the individual is at peace with the self, in relationships and with the world. To exercise the power of peace embraces the fundamental principle of spirituality; look inward in order to look outward with courage, purpose, and meaning. (*Living Values*)

Sit quietly alone with yourself somewhere for a few minutes. Think about what it is like to be near a deep, still ocean, where there is no wind and no noise. Enjoy that silence in your mind. This is your inner peace.

A BRAHMA KUMARIS VIEW OF WHAT IT MEANS TO BE FULLY HUMAN

The Brahma Kumaris World Spiritual University teaches a body of spiritual wisdom known as Raja Yoga. The teachings include an understanding of the self, the nature of God, the law of cause and effect and the cyclic nature of time. They are taught as practical methods for developing spiritual values in one's day-to-day life.

Four Aspects of a Fully Human Life

All human beings have a right to a life that is '*fully human*' which means a life lived to the fullest human potential. What are the implications of this? Life is a two way process, not just for taking but also very much for giving. To have a fully human life means to have a life filled with:

- Self-Understanding (Knowledge)
- Self Mastery (Inculcation)
- Relationship with God (Yoga)
- Serving Others (Service)

What do these concepts mean? How can they be achieved?

Self Understanding

Self understanding is about knowing yourself – your potential and strengths as well as your weaknesses. When you ask people if they love or even like themselves, often they say no. One reason for this is perhaps that we simply do not know ourselves well enough. However how will we be able to develop self-confidence if we do not know our own strengths and talents? How will we be able to use our talents to fulfil our potential in life?

Many people lack self-confidence because they feel that others do not appreciate them. However, it will be difficult to accept appreciation from others if you have not learned to appreciate and value your own self first. Inner, spiritual resources such as love, peace, happiness, wisdom and strength exist in us all, but they need to be used fully in order to live a fully human life. The more they are used, the greater the value we will have for ourselves. This, in turn, is what allows us to develop genuine self-esteem and confidence.

Our inner spiritual resources make up our true identity, as they are the qualities of the soul, not of the body alone.

The warmth and comfort of happiness is hidden within the self. Happiness does not carry a price tag. It cannot be bought, sold, or bargained for. Happiness is earned by those whose actions, attitudes and attributes are pure and selfless. In other words, the quality of the consciousness and activities of individuals determines the richness of life. (*Living Values*)

What gives you the most happiness? Is your happiness based on something that is in a state of change, or can you identify the stable and constant sources of happiness that are within the self?

This is about applying the universal principles governing human nature and conduct. Simply turning within will uncover those principles - those unbreakable, enduring, fundamental truths which transcend all belief systems. They are natural and spiritual laws (the knowledge of which) exists at the core of every human soul. They are concepts such as fairness and patience, honesty and integrity, benevolence and respect, accuracy and flexibility and all of the divine virtues which are part of our human potential (*Living Values*)

Think of a situation when you found it difficult to satisfy all the people involved. Applying these universal principles, how would you approach that situation now?

So many of the things we call our identity – name, nationality, profession – are connected to bodily appearance (skin colour, features, gender etc.) or to the role we play in life *through* the body, i.e. mother, sister, friend, teacher, housewife, lawyer and so on.

A body without a soul, or a soul without a body, cannot be considered fully human. The body needs a soul (or life force) within it to be alive or, you could say, fully human. To be fully human is to be aware that 'I' am the soul and that the body is my vehicle. It is a costume through which I play a role on the stage of the world. To be a soul means to be myself – something much greater than the roles that I play. Being a soul means that it is my inner qualities guiding me through life and not fear, insecurity, anger, prejudice and other negative feelings. I become free from these.

Self Mastery

Very often, people are negatively influenced by what others say or do. Circumstances, situations, even the weather can affect us this way. In fact, everything we see, hear, taste, touch and smell can have a powerful influence over us. When we are influenced, we react. The reaction may be one of anger or excitement. However in reacting, are we really using our power to choose? Self mastery is the ability to choose your attitudes, feelings, thoughts, words and actions. It means using soul awareness in your everyday life.

Relationship with God

To be fully human is to be in relationship with God. God is a source of truth, light, peace and love – a source of all that is good. God is beyond physical form and beyond the physical dimension. God can perhaps be thought of as a point source of energy for the whole universe, sustaining matter as well as the human soul. Our relationship with God is not dependent on anything physical but rather on the quality of our awareness. Awareness of the soul is what leads us to a relationship with God. By filling ourselves with all that is good from God, we become fully human; we become fulfilled. God becomes our parent, teacher, guide, friend and beloved. We remain constantly aware of God's love and protection even as we perform the most ordinary tasks.

Serving Others

It is a spiritual law that the more you give, the more you will receive. If you give with a true heart, in God's

13

This is about being so strong in my mind that I cannot become upset or distressed by anything that happens. If someone insults or criticises me then I am strong enough to listen and not become disheartened. I can learn instead. I can face any situation. Strength also means being able to achieve my goal. It is about having determination and faith in the self.

(Dadi Janki, Additional Administrative Head of the University.)

Which situation have you been strong in today? What are the major challenges that you have faced in your life? How did you find the strength to face these?

remembrance, then you will never be in need. Therefore, to be fully human is to serve others selflessly. To live life just for the self is to have a life devoid of meaning.

Sometimes it seems difficult to be giving in relationships, as others may interpret this as weakness, and try to take advantage of you. However, when your giving comes from a position of strength; that is, from a sense of self respect and discernment, then you can only gain. To give out of fear means to lose. To give with discernment means to give when you know that what you give will be valued and respected. We must remember our own value, and then give.

Make a list of all the roles that you play during one day. Think about how using your inner qualities can help you to play those roles better.

Make a list of 5 things that commonly influence you. What would your life be like if you were not influenced by these things?

Choose a relationship. Think about how that relationship would be if it were perfect. Think about how God could be that perfect relationship for you. What would be the benefit of this in your life?

When there is a situation of conflict with someone, try being the first one to give. For example if someone is angry, be loving instead of angry in return. If someone is jealous of you, especially try to make them your friend.

A BUDDHIST VIEW OF WHAT IT MEANS TO BE FULLY HUMAN

Manjusri Bodhisattva. In Mahayana Buddhism, a Bodhisattva is any being who out of compassion has taken a vow to become a Buddha for the sake of all sentient beings. Manjusri's name means Gentle Holy One, yet he also has a wrathful form as the Slayer of Death.

Not to commit evil

But to practise all good

And to keep the heart pure

This is the teaching of the Buddha

Dhammapada

This poem tells us how to be fully human in a Buddhist sense. In the Buddhist tradition, ethics or morality is considered one of the three trainings to cultivate, together with wisdom and compassion. The basis for Buddhist ethics is the five precepts: not to kill, not to steal, not to misuse sexuality, not to lie and not to take intoxicants. But these precepts are not seen as rules, they are considered like guidelines, to inspire us, to make us reflect, to help us cultivate compassion.

How can we cultivate these precepts?

We can refrain from doing something negative but more to the point we can practise the positive qualities of harmlessness, generosity, restraint, honesty and clarity. The precepts are to remind us that we live in a world with other people and that we have to consider ourselves and others equally. We need to care for ourselves and others. The root of Buddhist ethics is compassion.

Not to commit evil means not to cause suffering to ourselves or others.

How might we cause suffering? We can cause suffering through our body, speech and mind.

How do we act towards others? Do we use our body aggressively?

If we are bigger than someone else, do we use our extra strength to threaten others or make them do things they do not want to do. If we are clever with words, how do we use that ability? Do we humiliate people less intelligent or articulate than us?

Are we verbally aggressive?

Do we charm other people with words for an ulterior motive, for our own benefit, disregarding the suffering caused to them.

The thought manifests as the word;

The word manifests as the deed;

The deed develops into habit;

And habit hardens into character.

So watch the thought and its way with care,

And let it spring from love

Born out of concern for all beings.

The Buddha

Samantabhadra Bodhisattva, who protects all who teach *dharma*, the truth taught by the Buddha.

How do we use our own mind?

Do we cultivate resentment, hatred, judgement in our thoughts towards ourselves or others which would lead to suffering?

From a Buddhist point of view intention is very important.

Do we cause suffering accidentally, thoughtlessly or intentionally?

If we were to cause suffering intentionally that would be considered a bad intention. If it was from thoughtlessness, we would be told to cultivate awareness. If it was accidental, we would be encouraged to reflect on cause and effect. For example, what were the conditions that made the accident happen?

To practise all good means to cultivate the five precepts. It encourages us actively to cultivate harmlessness, that is think kindly, act kindly, speak kindly. It asks us to reflect on generosity. What do we want, how do we go about getting it?

Do we really need what we want?

Can we be generous towards people who have less than us or who need something from us? When it comes to the body and our desires and impulses, how do we act when they have us in their thrall?

Do we recognise the right of others?

Can we restrain our desires and impulses?

When we speak, can we speak with respect and care? Can we praise people instead of slandering them behind

The Birth of the Buddha.

The Lovely Avalokitesvara, the Bodhisattva of Compassion.

their back? Can we cultivate clarity and presence of mind by abstaining from taking intoxicants?

To keep the heart pure means to try to keep the mind uncluttered. If we seethe with resentment towards someone, plotting revenge, aren't we cluttering the mind with an endless obsession about that person? When we are constantly wanting things we cannot get, aren't we agitating our mind with endless craving?

How would it feel if our mind was quiet, spacious and contented, present with what is happening now and not troubled by past or future worries or desires?

To keep the heart pure does not mean that we are saintly. It means that we are reasonably aware, reasonably caring, open to ourselves and others, not influenced by hatred, greed or delusion.

This is the teaching of the Buddha means that the Buddhist way of life can be quite simple. It is not so much about going to a special place or reading profound books but about how do we act, think or speak today. Could it be more out of compassion than self-interest?

Questions

What do Buddhists say about the relationships between human beings and other living things?

How does that affect the way humans think and act?

A CHRISTIAN VIEW OF WHAT IT MEANS TO BE FULLY HUMAN

Many artists of different countries and in different centuries have painted the face of Jesus Christ. Christ Pantocrator, or Christ the Universal Lord, is from a seventh century portable icon from St Catherine's monastery, Sinai. The ecstatic expression of the face with the raised eyebrow is considered unique.
© *St Catherine's Monastery, Sinai*

So God created man in his own image, in the image of God he created him: male and female he created them. And God blessed them, and God said to them. "Be fruitful and multiply, and fill the earth and subdue it; and have dominion over the fish of the sea and over the birds of the air and over every living thing that moves upon the earth". And God said "Behold, I have given you every plant yielding seed ... for food." And God saw everything that he had made, and behold, it was very good. And there was evening and there was morning, a sixth day. Genesis 1:27-31

I cannot be human on my own. To be fully human means to be fully in relationship with others, the created world and God. This is joy. The fact that we are not fully human is our tragedy.

'In the beginning is relation,' wrote the Jewish philosopher Martin Buber. It is in the creation stories of Genesis, the first book of the Bible and scripture for both Jews and Christians, that the contours of relation are outlined. In Genesis chapter 1 each day of creation ends 'And God saw that it was good'. Then on the sixth day, in the creation of humans, right relationships are described: man and woman made in the image of God, called to be fruitful and to multiply, with dominion over every animal and with plants for food. The sixth day ends 'and behold it was very good.'

Humans, in the next creation story in Genesis, are placed in the garden of Eden. Gardening is humans working with nature, to 'till and keep it'. 'It is not good for man to be alone' leads God to the creation of woman. All humans are symbolically descended from Adam and Eve. We are at the very least all cousins, members of one extended family.

We cannot be fully human without God, each other and the rest of creation. And the story of the fall, the disobedience of Adam and Eve, is the story of the fall from right relationships. The immediate consequence of this fall is that pain in childbirth shall be multiplied, the husband shall rule over the wife, bread be obtained by hard work and death shall return us to dust. Then comes the story of one son murdering the other.

Yet without the freedom to choose, humans cannot be fully human. To be fully human is a project in which humans must freely participate. God cannot make us fully human without our consent and commitment.

Evidence of the 'fall' is all around us. Family violence has not ended. Both domestic violence, terrorism and war are daily in the news. For many no matter how hard they work, there is not enough bread or rice. This last twentieth century has been called a century of progress and death. The Jewish holocaust has been described as not the end of history but the beginning of the end. The Nazis took the Jews to the ovens in Auschwitz and other death camps, but the Allies in their bombing raids later in World War II, took the ovens to the civilians in Germany and Japan. The dropping of the atom bomb on Hiroshima and Nagasaki has brought us to the precipice. Ethnic cleansing in the former Yugoslavia, genocide in Rwanda, and an expanding club of nations with nuclear weapons indicate we are still at the precipice.

18

A Japanese artist's picture of the face of Jesus. ©*World Council of Churches*

Jesus said: I am come that they might have life and have it more abundantly.

John 10:10

From the Sermon on the Mount:

"Blessed are those who are persecuted for righteousness' sake, for theirs is the kingdom of heaven.

'Love your enemies.'

'Do not lay up for yourselves treasures upon earth ...'

Matthew 5:10, 44, 6:19

If the fall is the last chapter of the human story then there is no hope for us. But for Christians there is another chapter – called redemption, restoration. Its setting is among the Jewish people who experienced redemption from slavery in Egypt, with a new constitution for a new kind of society, in the giving of the law at Mount Sinai. God is redeemer as well as creator. There is a vision among the prophets of a new day, a redeemed day for all humanity. Isaiah, for instance, speaks of an end to war and a return to the paradise of Eden with the lion eating straw like the ox (Isaiah 2:1–4, 11:1–9). God's agent of redemption will be the Messiah.

For Christians Jesus of Nazareth is the Messiah. and more than Messiah. He is 'God with us' (Matthew 2:23). To look at Jesus is to see how 'in him all the fullness of God was pleased to dwell' (Colossians 1:19). Jesus translates what God is like into human language and life. To see Jesus is to see the Father (John 14:9). Jesus is God.

But Jesus is also human and the measure of what it means to be fully human. It is not to be born privileged, nor to aspire after greatness, riches or power. It is in fact to give up and renounce all these ambitions and live and die as a servant who loves others. To be fully human is to risk the pain of relationship with others. Jesus' challenge to his disciples, to take up their cross and follow him, was a challenge to be vulnerable. His teaching, particularly in the Sermon on the Mount (Matthew 5–7), describes how to risk being vulnerable disciples.

Jesus calls for decision. We are not fully human unless we are decisive about how we should live. Someone who just drifts or follows the crowd is not fully human.

Just as I cannot be fully human on my own, so I cannot be Christian by myself. When Paul describes Christians as members of the body of Christ with Christ as the head (1 Corinthians 12), he is describing how Christians are Christians only in relationship to each other and to Christ. I cannot be a solo Christian.

To be fully human is to live vulnerably for others. The fact that Christians have not always done this – to our condemnation – indicates that the fall remains very powerful and that redemption is not yet complete.

According to Genesis everything in the beginning was created 'good'. Does this mean we can ultimately trust the Universe and Nature?

What does 'the fall' mean?

Why is the cross important for Christians in their search to become fully human?

How do people become fully human according to Christian teachings?

A HINDU VIEW OF WHAT IT MEANS TO BE FULLY HUMAN

When totally free from outer contacts a man finds happiness in himself,

he is fully trained in God's discipline and reaches unending bliss.

The experiences we owe to our sense of touch are only sources of unpleasantness.

They have a beginning and an end.

A wise man takes no pleasure in them.

That man is disciplined and happy who can prevail over the turmoil that springs from desire and anger, here on earth, before he leaves his body.

Bhagavad Gita 5.21–23

Smaller than the smallest, greater than the greatest, this Self forever dwells within the hearts of all. When a man is free from desire, his mind and senses purified, he beholds the glory of the Self and is without sorrow.

Though seated, he travels far; though at rest, he moves all things. Who but the purest of the pure can realize this Effulgent Being, who is joy and who is beyond joy?

Formless is he, though inhabiting form. In the midst of the fleeting he abides forever. All-pervading and supreme is the Self. The wise man, knowing him in his true nature, transcends all grief.

Katha Upanishad 1.2.20–22

Hindu ideas are based on enormously varied concepts of visible and invisible links between all individual beings and the larger cosmic sphere. Realising this interlinkedness makes a person human, i.e. aware of his or her place in this cosmos. Understanding of such links distinguishes the best human beings from those who merely look like humans but act like animals.

Such concepts of linkage also involve a constant evaluation of all human actions in terms of *dharma* (individual duty to do the appropriate thing at the right time) and *karma* (automatic consequences of any action or non-action, thus retribution).

Depending on an individual's viewpoint and perspective, certain actions are perceived to be more meritorious than others. Generally speaking, a fully human life involves knowing one's place and taking responsibility for one's own actions while taking account of the needs of others. The key issue here is awareness of what one does, or realisation of the invisible links, for the consequences of actions still come about, whether one is aware of them or not. Thus, awareness of the ethical dimension of life is an indicator of civilisation and of being a Hindu while those humans who do not understand the Hindu interlinkedness have been conceived of as 'barbarians', not fully human people.

Because Hinduism does not draw a strict borderline between the human race, gods, and the animal and plant worlds, Hindu literature offers much material on what a fully human existence means: doing one's job in one's place, doing the right thing at the right time, without only thinking about oneself. Basically, this encourages altruism rather than selfish egoism, it is idealistic, but it remains very real.

The six sections of the Global Ethic are seen as interlinked from the perspective of Hindu traditions and those religions influenced by them. To describe a complex field of this kind in a few words seems a more difficult task than analysing it, since description has to proceed step by step on little points, whereas analysis can immediately grapple with the big key issues.

Bright but hidden, the Self dwells
in the heart

Everything that moves, breathes,
opens and closes

Lives in the Self. He is the source
of love

And may be known through love
but not through thought

He is the goal of life. Attain this
goal!

The shining Self dwells hidden in
the heart.

Everything in the cosmos, great
and small,

Lives in the Self. He is the source
of life,

Truth beyond the transience of this
world.

He is the goal of life. Attain this goal!

Mundaka Upanishad, 2.

May your counsel be common,
your assembly common, common
the mind, and the thoughts of
these united.

A common purpose do I lay before
you, and worship with your
common oblation.

Let your aims be common, and
your hearts of one accord, and all
of you be of one mind, so you may
live well together.

Rig Veda 10.191.2-4

Let us have concord with our own
people, and concord with people
who are strangers to us;

May we unite in our minds, unite
in our purposes, and not fight
against the divine spirit within us.

Atharva Veda 7.52.1-2

The analytical key issue in all of this is the interlinkedness of any little individual with everything else in the world. Hinduism has been very clear about this from very early on, but has developed quite different approaches to making this interlinkedness work. The danger, from a self-critical Hindu perspective, is that Hindus assume that their own tradition stands for global ethics, the familiar old story of cultural superiority. If we are debating this now, what do we make of the fact that the same issues were debated thousands of years ago among Hindus?

The way in which the issues have been presented in the Global Ethic in a certain order seems to reflect a particular cultural/religious agenda rather than a global perspective. It may be impossible to discuss such a global perspective without making reference to any one tradition, whether explicitly or implicitly. However, the emphasis in the text on 'do not kill', 'do not steal', 'do not lie' etc. seems too Christian-inspired, so that it will be necessary to comment on various issues from a Hindu perspective.

Questions

Can one rank living beings on the basis of their capacity for awareness?

Can you think of an illustration of full humanity expressed in doing a job well?

A JEWISH VIEW OF WHAT IT MEANS TO BE FULLY HUMAN

To be fully human is to be in the image of God.

Judaism believes that the Bible prescribes certain minimum standards of behaviour for all human beings. All human beings now, according to the Bible, are descended from Noah, whose family were the only ones to survive the Great Flood. Therefore these commandments are known as the Commandments of the Children of Noah.

1. Do not worship idols.
2. Do not blaspheme against God.
3. Establish a just legal system in the society in which you live.
4. Do not murder.
5. Do not commit adultery or incest.
6. Do not steal.
7. Do not eat flesh taken from a living animal.

Judaism also has attempted to find some way of summarising all Jewish teaching, in rather the way the Global Ethic summarises the ethical teaching of all the world. One such summary is this one from the Talmud, which records the debates of the teachers of Judaism in Babylon before 600 CE.

'R.Simlai when preaching said: Six hundred and thirteen commandments were given to Moses. David came and reduced them to eleven principles, as it is written, A Psalm of David, Eternal, who shall sojourn in Your tabernacle? Who shall dwell in Your holy mountain? – (i) Those that walk uprightly, and (ii) work righteousness, and (iii) speak truth in their heart; that (iv) have no slander upon their tongues, (v) nor do evil to others, (vi) nor reproach their neighbours, (vii) in whose eyes a vile person is despised, but (viii) who honour them that fear the Eternal, (ix) They swear truthfully, even if this damages their own interests and do not change, (x) They do not put out their money on interest, (xi) nor take a bribe against the innocent. Those who do these things shall never be moved. (Psalm 15)

Micah came and reduced them to three principles, as it is written, It has been told you what is good, and what the Eternal requires of you: (i) only to do justly, and (ii) to love mercy and (iii) to walk humbly before your God. 'To do justly,' that is, maintaining justice; 'and to love mercy' that is, doing every kindness; 'and walking humbly before your God,' that is, walking in funeral and bridal processions . . .

Again came Isaiah and reduced them to two principles, as it is said, Thus says the Eternal, (i) Keep justice and (ii) do righteousness (etc.) Amos came and reduced them to one principle, as it is said, For thus says the Eternal unto the house of Israel, Seek Me and live. But it is Habakuk who came and based them all on one principle, as it is said, 'But the righteous shall live by his faith.'

There are several stories in Jewish teaching which try to make clear the value all human beings should put on the lives of another.

A man came to his teacher and said, 'The king says that I must kill a certain man, or he will put me to death. Shall I put him to death to save my own life? 'No' said Rava his teacher, 'For how do you know that your blood is redder than his? (Babylonian Talmud, Pesachim).

A later code proclaimed, *If one person is able to save another and does not save them, that is a refusal to obey the commandment, Do not stand idly by the blood of your neighbour.* (Maimonides, Mishnah Torah).

While you must do everything you can to save your neighbour, that can mean sacrificing your own life for him, but that is not an obligation.

If you and someone else are lost in the desert and you have one bottle of water which only contains enough to get one person to safety, do you share the water with your companion, in which case you both die, or do you keep the water bottle for yourself, so one at least survives? The rabbis decided that you may keep all the water for yourself. To give the water bottle to your companion would be an act of great kindness, but it is not compulsory. But it is forbidden for you to share the water because that would lead to both of you dying. (Babylonian Talmud, Baba Metziah).

At a time when most people in the world thought disliking those from other countries and religions absolutely normal, William Shakespeare wrote about recognising the human value of those very different from ourselves.

I am a Jew. Hath not a Jew eyes. Hath not a Jew hands, organs, dimensions, senses, affections, passions, fed with the same food, hurt with the same weapons, subject to the same diseases, healed by the same means, warmed and cooled by the same winter and summer as a Christian is? If you prick us, do we not bleed? If you tickle us, do we not laugh? If you poison us, do we not die?

The early teachers of Judaism debated whether human beings should have been created. Some of them felt that there was so much suffering in the world that perhaps life is not worth living. Others felt that life is worth living and the greatest glory of human beings is that we can work with God to perfect this world and create a time when there is no war or pain in the world and everyone lives in harmony.

Questions:

1. We believe that God is not limited by physical space, eternal, omniscient. Human beings are limited to physical bodies, live for only a limited period and do not know everything, or even remember everything they have known? In what way are human beings in God's image?

2. Does our society reflect the values of the Commandments of the Children of Noah?

3. Are there any commandments you would want to add to the seven Commandments of the Children of Noah to make a basic ethical system? Are there any you would want to remove?

4. What key principles of Jewish teaching are important in the summary of all the commandments?

5. What do Jews believe to be the role of humanity in this world?

6. Do you agree that it might be better for human beings not to have been created?

7. The Bible says that you must love your neighbour as yourself. A later Jewish teacher said that you should not do to others what you would not like done to you. Which of these do you think is the better rule?

8. What does the story mean when it asks, 'Is your blood redder than his?'

9. Can you think of examples of 'standing idly by the blood of your neighbour'?

A MUSLIM VIEW OF WHAT IT MEANS TO BE FULLY HUMAN

The very creation of the heavens and of the earth are signs of His, and the diversity of your languages and colour - signs, truly, for all that lives.

Other signs, again, are in the daily, nightly habit of sleep, and all your acquisitive pursuit of His good things - signs at least for people who give heed to them.

Again, there are signs from Him in the lightning you see, inspiring fear and yearning, and in the rain that pours from heaven with which He rouses the dead land into life - signs, that is, for people who use their minds.

There are signs, yet again, in the very stability of the heavens and of the earth, by His authority, and signs, too, in that when His summons calls you from the earth, forth you will come.

To Him belongs all that is, in the heavens and in the earth, each and all subservient to his Will. He it is who initiates creation and continually renews it - a light task for Him! For supreme excellence is His, in the heavens and in the earth: He is the Lord of might and wisdom.

Qu'ran 30.22-27

'In relation to the creator Muslims are absolutely identical in their creatureliness'. Riadh el Droubie.

For a Muslim to be fully human means being conscious of God and worshipping Him and observing the rules of conduct enshrined in His revealed book, the Holy Qur'an. The message of the Qur'an outlines human responsibilities to other people as members of families, communities and human beings.

A Muslim is any male or female who consciously and solemnly witnesses that 'there is no God but God and that Muhammad is the Prophet of God'. All things in the world of the Qur'an begin, continue and end in God. Praise is the due recognition by humans of God's sovereignty and the Muslim constantly remembers that 'God is most great'.

The world, created by God, gives many signs of God's goodness and should be a constant reminder to human beings of their dependence on and gratitude to God.

Human beings are called to be God's vice-regents, caring for the world God has entrusted to them.

Although to be a Muslim requires confession of faith in God and His prophet, Islam believes that God judges people by their deeds, not by ceremonies or creeds. Every Muslim should pursue a righteous life, because God created human beings to do good deeds. The Qur'an pictures the life of humans as a free competition to do noble deeds.

Your God is one God: there is no god but He, the merciful Lord of mercy.

For a people who think intelligently there are signs in the creation of the heavens and of the earth, in the alternation of night and day, in the ships which voyage on the seas to the profit of mankind, in the waters God sends down from the heavens giving life out of lifelessness to the earth, in the population of the earth with every kind of living creature, in the hither and thither of winds and clouds harnessed to His purposes between sky and land.

Qu'ran 2.163–164

God has given you the sea for seamanship: by his leave the ships ply freely as you go after His good things. Perhaps you will be grateful.

Indeed, He has put to your service all things in the heavens and in the earth. All are His, and truly in all there are signs for reflective people.

Qu'ran 45.12–14

'Muslims have a feeling of strong brotherhood to all who submit themselves to the Divine Sovereign; for in relation to the Creator, there is no perspective or bond mightier and more proper than that of being human creatures. Here all humans stand absolutely identical in their *creatureliness*. On account of their acknowledgement of God alone as Master, Muslims are revolutionaries who champion the cause of human freedom against *human* masters everywhere. Nothing is more hateful to them than associating other beings with God. When people set up money, sex, power, or pleasure as their God beside God, it is deplorable. But when a tyrant sets himself up and demands absolute loyalty from the citizens – loyalty belonging exclusively to God – then rebellion against that ruler and his ultimate overthrow become, for the Muslims, a prime religious objective.'

From *Islam* by Isma'il R Al Faruqi, p. 7

Questions

How should a Muslim behave as a vice-regent of God?

How do you think a strong belief in a future life, either of reward or punishment, affects how you behave?

A RASTAFARIAN VIEW OF WHAT IT MEANS TO BE FULLY HUMAN

Ras Tafari - Emperor Haile Selassie.

Ras Tafari is the given name of His Imperial Majesty Emperor Haile Selassie I prior to his coronation as Negust Negast (King of Kings) on the 2 November 1930. In Amharic, Ras literally translates as King or Head and Tafari is the given name of His Imperial Majesty. Haile Selassie translates as Might of the Trinity. The worship of His Imperial Majesty Emperor Haile Selassie I, Jah Rastafari, as God the holy King of Creation is a fundamental tenet of Rastafarian doctrine. The doctrine symbolically represents the rebirth of the African people, who were enslaved in the Americas and the Caribbean, between the fifteenth and nineteenth centuries and systematically deprived of their religious practices, culture, customs, belief systems, national identity, language and dignity.

Out of this history of inhumanity, Rastafarian doctrine has developed as a philosophy of peace and love, in which all human life is considered sacred, irrespective of race, gender, age, physical or mental impairment, or state of grace. Indeed, most Rastafarians view all life as sacred. This is reflected in many having strict vegetarian diets, eating only ital (pure) foods. Some Rastas argue that plants are sacred and when eating any life form, be it plant or animal, one should give thanks first of all to Jah Rastafari, the creator of all things and then to the life force being consumed for the ultimate sacrifice it makes in giving the essence of its life for man's sustenance.

Rasta doctrine dictates respect for the wonders of Jah's creation – Life, the Universe, the Cosmos, Mother Earth, or whatever one may wish to call it. For Rastafarians, life begins at the moment of conception and the foetus is a living being at all stages of its development. Needless to say, most Rastafarians are opposed to abortion, which is generally viewed as murder. As a matter of fact, birth control is widely considered as an attempt to destroy the African race and to maintain Western/white supremacy. In the Rastafarian view this is confirmed by the seeming Western emphasis on birth control to solve the problems of the 'Third World', thereby ignoring racial, economic and other social inequalities, which Rastafarians view as the roots of their oppression. In contrast there seems to be an increasing Western interest in developing sophisticated technology to enhance their own fertility. Given the historical fact of the mass enslavement and annihilation of millions of Africans on the African continent and in the diaspora, many Rastafarians see an increased African birth rate as being the only way of preserving the African peoples from extinction.

In this regard the family as a unit is fundamental to Rastafarian doctrine and, being governed by the dictates of the Bible, the philosophy of Rastafari places paramount importance on children and young people within the movement. This is in line with the injunction of Christ in the Book of Matthew (18:2–7), that unless one were to become as a little child one would never be able to enter the Kingdom of Heaven and that 'anyone who is an obstacle to bring down one of these little ones who have faith in me would be better drowned in the depths of the sea with a great millstone around his neck'. This importance is again emphasised in the Book of Proverbs (13:22) where it states that 'a good man bequeaths his heritage to his children's children'.

For Rastas, children are to be loved, cherished and accorded the status of royal princes and princesses. The love of Rastafarians for their children is well renowned and is clearly a prime inspiration in the creative works of Rastafarian artists and musicians. The paintings of Ras Daniel Hartmen depict the royal status of Rastafarian children and the unity and love between Rastafarians and their children. Rastafarian children are raised to live in accordance with the moral dictates of the lifestyle of the Rastafarian movement. They are encouraged to be proud of their African heritage and to seek truth through good deeds, constant study of the Bible and of history. Rastafarians are enjoined to humble themselves to the level of little children so that they may enter the Kingdom of Heaven-Zion Ethiopia. This love also reflects the role of His Imperial Majesty Emperor Haile Selassie I Jah Rastafari as God the father who cares for humanity as a father cares for his children.

The essential of human life being sacred is based on the premise that, upon conception, the 'I' or 'Godliness' of the Creator Jah Rastafari is imbued within the living entity. We are all born as Rastas. As such, the body is viewed as the living essence of Jah, as we were created in his image. It is the living 'Temple of Jah', which has to be respected at all times. The Rastafarian concept of 'I' is one of inner-God consciousness. The term 'I and I' is the collective. 'I' is considered to be 'Man', a state of inner one-ness with Jah. Out of this state one moves into the realm of wickedness and becomes 'Men'. 'I' or righteousness is eternal life, whilst wickedness is death. Hence many Rastafarians view 'Men' (the wicked) as the 'living dead'. However, even this absence from Jah does not prevent one from attaining a state of 'I Man-one-ness with Jah' by constant prayer, meditation and good works. Every action has an opposite reaction. In many ways this is similar to the Hindu concepts of Dharma and Karma. Rastafarian doctrine dictates that we live by doing good and having good come to us in return.

Insofar as the ways of Babylon (the West) are seen to be evil and destructive, the goal of many Rastas is to leave Babylon and return to Mother Africa. This entails returning to the source and becoming one with nature, moving with the flow of the seasons away from the destructive Western technological pollution and exploitation of the planet. In this state of grace Rastas become one with the earth, with a respect for the whole of humanity. This extends even to those who have entered the state of becoming 'Men' (wicked). The Rastafarian universe is based on the premise that in the plan of Creation the human family was intended to live in a state of 'Inity' (unity). However, to move away from the 'inity' can only result in ultimate physical and spiritual death. Insofar as the African people have historically been enslaved, subjugated, brutalised, brainwashed and systematically deprived of their religious practices, cultures, customs, belief systems, national identities, languages and dignity – the collective prayer of Rastafari is for the ultimate destruction of the wicked and this unjust system of oppression. Hence a return to the ways of nature and one-ness with Jah – a state of 'I Man'.

Questions

In what ways do the Rastafarians express their respect for the wonders of creation?

Why do many Rastas return to Africa?

16

A SIKH VIEW OF WHAT IT MEANS TO BE FULLY HUMAN

In many lives, became insects and moths;

In many lives, became elephant, fish and deer;

In many lives, became bird and snake;

In many lives, became yoked horse and ox;

This is your turn to meet God, the Lord of All.

This human body has been shaped after a long wait.

Guru Arjan: *Guru Granth Sahib* GGS-176

O my mind, you are the embodiment of God's light

Remember your root!

GGS-441

O my body, God installed the light in you

That is why you came into the world.

Guru Amardas: GGS-921

Sikhism teaches that God created all life and there is a special place for human beings. As can be seen from the verses in column 1, Guru Arjan, the fifth Guru, has described this relationship as working towards a human life form through transmigration into many different lives of birds and animals.

Sikhs believe that one becomes separated from our divine source as a result of his/her actions, and it is necessary to get back to that divine source. The human life is therefore, very precious in which we have the opportunity to choose to live in a way which helps us to rediscover our divine origin. This is the foremost goal for a human being.

We are all part of the divine as the divine light shines in all of us. Guru Amardas, the third Guru, told us that we come into this world when God puts that light in us.

Therefore it is our duty to ensure that we do not forget that precious light which exists within each one of us. The human soul is fundamentally an image of the divine, but a person considers himself/herself as separate because he/she creates a wall of self-centredness (*haumai*, literally Me First), around himself/herself. When that wall of self-centredness demolishes, then the human becomes one with God. In other words, human life is not a prison, or a trapping net, but a way of achieving the spiritual goal. A fully human life is, therefore, a life of responsibility to God and to fellow human beings and other creatures.

There are three aspects of a human being. They are:

body
mind
soul

A human being needs to develop all three. The human body needs to be cared for because the soul resides within it. This body is the temple of the divine. It is important for its nurturing and looking after that a grown up person earns a living and observes the rules of healthy living, for self and family. For the development of the mind, learning and sound education are necessary.

28

You have been blessed with the human body

Your time to meet the divine Sovereign

All other tasks are of no value,

Except to join the Society of spiritual people

And meditate.

Be prepared to swim across the tortuous world ocean

You are wasting your life in worldly pleasures

Have not practised meditation, Self-discipline and responsibility,

Not been of service, nor served holy people or recognised the divine.

Nanak says, 'My deeds are mean, O God!

I seek your shelter, Save my honour.'

Guru Arjan: GGS-12

Education helps us to understand the deeper meaning of life and of nature around us. For the development of the soul, it is necessary that an individual leads a moral life according to a religious and spiritual path. One's spiritual development assists in achieving salvation from the cycle of birth and death, and to merge with God at the end of human life.

Sikhs also believe that God has made human beings in charge of the earth, and other life forms that exist here. As God's stewards' we have a responsibility of care and conservation, and not that of exploitation.

In Sikhism there is much in common with other faiths. We all share the same environment and have responsibility towards each other, other people of faith and also those who have no faith. The Sikhs also believe that the divine does not cease to be divine because in our human frailties we lose faith. The cultivation of the inner spirit and of service to fellow beings are important in a Sikh's view of life. Without these there is no full and fulfilling human life. Therefore a fully human life is a life of meditation and prayer, self-discipline, service and responsibility to others.

Ideas for exploration

1. Sikhs believe that a human being comes from God and should work to return there. What are the reasons for this belief?

2. Is *haumai* a good thing? If not, why not?

3. How can we become fully human according to the Sikh teachings?

A ZORASTRIAN VIEW OF WHAT IT MEANS TO BE FULLY HUMAN?

If ye, O Mortals, realize and understand the laws of happiness and pain ordained by Mazda; and if you learn that liars and wicked persons shall face age long punishment but pious and righteous ones shall enjoy ever-lasting prosperity, then you shall reach real contentment and salvation, by learning this principle.

Gathic Yasna (GY) 30,11

Listen with your ears to the highest truths, consider them with illumined minds carefully and decide each man and woman personally between the two paths, good and evil. Before the ushering in of the great day, or the day of judgement, arise all of you and try to spread Ahuras words

(Zarathusthra's message).

The twain spirits which appeared in the world of thought in the beginning were good and evil in thoughts, words and deeds. The wise will choose rightly (of the said two thoughts), but the unwise shall not do so and shall go astray.

GY 30, 2 & 3.

The average Zoroastrian does not go around thinking 'Am I acting in a fully human way?' She/he has probably never even thought very deeply about the matter. However, despite the absence of conscious consideration of the question, the upbringing of a young Zoroastrian by Zoroastrian parents will reflect the values and norms which represent and are acceptable within the Zoroastrian community. In this way members of the community absorb the notions of what it is to be a full member of society, and thus fully human, without necessarily having to be sat down and taught principles. Lessons can be learnt passively, just from copying the social conventions of those around. Nevertheless conversations in Zoroastrian households often touch on moral choices and ethical issues and thus children from a young age become familiar with the vocabulary dealing with concepts of right and wrong choice, if not with the concepts themselves. This teaching is formally recognized in the initiation ceremony *sedreh pushi* conducted at an age when the ability to reason is thought to have developed in a child.

A fully human life consists of a rounded experience during a lifetime which is more than that merely shared with the animal kingdom. Of course in common with our fellow creatures we eat, we reproduce, we age, we die. However, we think there is something unique to humans which differentiates us from other animals, even the higher primates. One of the dimensions of this 'something' is a conscience. Zoroastrians are made aware of their conscience at a very early age through their parents' discussions about moral choices which they have to make throughout their growing lives and as suggested above, their awareness is enhanced by the prominent discussions of what it is to be a Zoroastrian. It is not just ethnic difference but a different morality which makes a Zoroastrian feel Zoroastrian rather than a member of another community within human society. Intrinsic to that, is the ability to weigh up the moral rectitude according to the dictates of *conscience*, which in turn provides one of the essential criteria for a fully **human** as opposed to a merely animal life. A key verse in the *Gathas* (the principal Zoroastrian text) exhorts each individual to heed the voice of conscience and to make free decisions rather than to be forced into them by external pressures.

Mazda Ahura, the Absolute Ruler, has specified that good fortune is for him who makes others happy.

In truth, the person who shows us the path of truth and happiness in the corporeal world and saves our soul in the spiritual one shall attain the highest good. The said path is that which leads us to the real and true world, where there is Ahura.

GY 43, 1 & 3

Those persons would enjoy that precious reward which has been promised, O Mazda, who perform actions through knowledge and pure thought; who strive for the progress and development of the world; fulfil God's desire and try for the progress of God's Will through truth and righteousness.

GY 34,14

In practical terms, the heightened awareness of conscience developed in Zoroastrian children is maintained by repeating the adage which enshrines Zoroastrian thinking: 'Good thoughts, good words, good deeds'. The translation of this into action is a striving to leave the world a better place through deeds which you have initiated, or at the very least to minimise the negative impact of your actions. To live a fully human life is to have the freedom to enjoy and live in harmony with the earth created by the Wise Lord and with all the manifestations of His creations emanating from His creative spirit. This freedom is a right of all humans, but it is an extremely delicate balancing act to enjoy your freedom without limiting the freedom of others. Thus to enjoy a fully human life you also have to take account of other creatures and of the impact your actions will have on the life of others. Again it is your *conscience* which will guide you to choose the path of truth and righteousness (**asha**.)

The Zoroastrian outlook is optimistic and confident, since it presumes that humans are naturally inclined towards goodness and that the general sum of goodness will prevail, if only people will follow the path of righteousness and purity in thought, word and deed. Clarity of mind to perceive which is indeed the path of righteousness (**asha**) may be achieved by purity of the physical environment around you.

Questions

What are the characteristics that make humans different from animals?

How do you recognize the voice of conscience ?

31

SECTION C

C. 1

The First Directive is:

Commitment to a culture of non-violence and respect for life

A BAHA'I VIEW OF COMMITMENT TO A CULTURE OF NON-VIOLENCE AND RESPECT FOR LIFE

Ye were created to show love one to another and not perversity and rancour. Take pride not in love for yourselves but in love for your fellow-creatures.

Baha'u'llah, *Tablets of Baha'u'llah* 138

He Who is your Lord, the All-Merciful, cherisheth in His heart the desire of beholding the entire human race as one soul and one body.

Baha'u'llah, *Gleanings* 214

Concentrate all the thoughts of your heart on love and unity. When a thought of war comes, oppose it by a stronger thought of peace. A thought of hatred must be destroyed by a more powerful thought of love. Thoughts of war bring destruction to all harmony, well-being, restfulness and content. Thoughts of love are constructive of brotherhood, peace, friendship and happiness.

'Abdu'l-Baha, *Paris Talks* 29

True civilization will come only when the leaders of nations, motivated solely by what is for the good and happiness of all people, agree to Peace, and set up a world-wide system to establish and maintain it. Such a peace must be upheld by firm treaties and methods of dealing with disputes and aggressive action between nations.

This, however, will need the backing of all humankind. The personal attitude and behaviour of the individual is the basis of a peaceful world, and every person must consider it his or her sacred duty to support and uphold that Peace. Our purpose in our own lives is to promote peaceful relationships with others.

Which qualities promote peaceful relationships with others?	
perversity and bitter hate	tolerance and love
separation from others	unity with others
love for yourself only	love for fellow creatures
love for just your own country or race	love for all humankind
intolerance between religions	acceptance of other views

There are copious references in the Baha'i Writings to all humankind making up one people. Baha'u'llah commands us to regard all humanity as: one soul and one body, the flowers of one garden, the fruits of one tree, the waves of one sea, members of one family. Even further, not only should we love humankind, but are instructed to "act towards all living creatures with justice and equity".

The education of women, and women's full participation in decision and policy-making in world affairs is an essential requirement for lasting peace. The Baha'i Writings state 'In past ages humanity has been defective and inefficient because it has been incomplete.' The education of women will be 'a mighty step' towards the abolition and ending of war as women will not permit their children to be sacrificed in battle. 'In truth, she (woman) will be the greatest factor in establishing universal peace and international arbitration. Assuredly, woman will abolish warfare among mankind.'

('Abdu'l-Baha, *Promulgation of Universal Peace*, 108)

War is destruction, while Universal Peace is construction; war is death while peace is life; war is rapacity and bloodthirstiness while peace is beneficence and humaneness; ... war is darkness upon darkness while peace is heavenly light; war is the destroyer of the edifice of mankind while peace is the everlasting life of the world of humanity; war is like a devouring wolf while peace is like the angels of heaven; war is the struggle for existence while peace is mutual aid and co-operation among the peoples of the world and the cause of the good pleasure of the True One in the heavenly realm.

'Abdu'l-Baha, *Baha'i Peace Programme* 11

Even economically violence is a bad option for the world. War only wastes lives and resources. The earth's wealth should be put to uses that profit humankind.

IMAGINE how we could improve our world if each nation used its resources for good, rather than aggression and defence

EITHER	OR
destruction of villages or cities	suitable living conditions
wastage on weapons of war	resources used to improve life
research/inventions used to destroy	research/inventions used to improve life
destruction of natural environment	preservation of the natural environment

---

THINK more about further spin-offs – for example:

- increased attitudes of justice towards all living creatures

- less need for military and law-enforcement forces; personnel can work in more productive areas.

A Baha'i Prayer for Peace and Unity

The well-being of mankind, its peace and security, are unobtainable unless and until its unity is firmly established. This unity can never be achieved so long as the counsels which the Pen of the Most High hath revealed are suffered to pass unheeded.

Baha'u'llah, *Gleanings* 286

O kind Lord! Thou Who art generous and merciful! We are the servants of Thy threshold and we are under the protection of Thy mercy. The Sun of Thy providence is shining upon all and the clouds of Thy mercy shower upon all. Thy gifts encompass all, Thy providence sustains all, Thy protection overshadows all and the glances of Thy favour illumine all. O Lord! Grant unto us Thine infinite bestowals and let Thy light of guidance shine. Illumine the eyes, make joyous the souls and confer a new spirit upon the hearts. Give them eternal life. Open the doors of Thy knowledge; let the light of faith shine. Unite and bring mankind into one shelter beneath the banner of Thy protection, so that they may become as waves of one sea, as leaves and branches of one tree, and may assemble beneath the shadow of the same tent. May they be refreshed by the same breezes. May they obtain illumination from the same source of light and life. Thou art the Giver, the Merciful!

'Abdu'l-Baha

A BRAHMA KUMARIS VIEW OF COMMITMENT TO A CULTURE OF NON-VIOLENCE AND RESPECT FOR LIFE

Respect is an acknowledgment of the inherent worth and innate rights of the individual and the collective. These must be recognised as the central focus to draw from people a commitment to a higher purpose in life. International respect and recognition for intellectual rights and originality of ideas must be observed without discrimination. The eminence of life is present in everyone, and every human being has a right to the joy of living with respect and dignity. (Living Values)

Respect for others is the result of spiritual awareness. With spiritual awareness, I recognise the efforts of those around me to improve themselves. This encourages me to focus more on the potential and unique specialities of my companions, rather than on their faults. In fact, this is the method to help people be free from their faults. I can judge the quality of my spiritual awareness by seeing how much faith I have in the ultimate transformation of my companions. This faith and love is true respect. (Companion of God)

Is it possible to have a world which is free of all suffering and a sense of peacelessness? Today, violence and war can be witnessed in every corner of this planet. Violence often appears in the workplace and in the home. Is it just part of human nature to be this way? Or is a better way of life truly possible for the people of our planet?

Within the Brahma Kumaris' teachings, such a non-violent world is definitely possible and achievable. The first step in this is to recognize the difference between non-violence and violence. Because we immediately witness the suffering it causes, physical aggression is easily recognisable as violence. Words spoken out of anger or hatred are also violence. The pain caused by words can last for years or even a lifetime. However, one who is violent towards others, is first violent towards their own self. This is a more subtle, fundamental form of violence, which needs to be understood.

Self-Violence

Self-violence is the first violence. It occurs when the original qualities of the self (love, peace, happiness, wisdom, strength) are not allowed to come into expression. The following states of being block these original qualities:

- Lack of self-respect
- Lack of faith in the self
- Lack of self-value
- Depression
- Selfishness
- Fear of others
- Looking towards people, possessions or circumstances to provide your sense of happiness.

To become non-violent, we first have to develop positive and loving thoughts towards the self, so that we value ourselves deeply and feel a deep, inner sense of well being. When these original qualities are encouraged to come into expression, there can no longer be any violence towards the self, or others.

Practise developing an attitude of non-violence towards the self. See how this affects your relationships with others.

36

**Developing Non-Violence
Towards the Self (A Meditation)**

**Developing Non-Violence
Towards the Self (A Meditation)**

The Brahma Kumaris believe that everyone has the potential to be non-violent. Here is a pattern of meditation which they recommend.

Please say these words quietly, slowly and gently to the self:

I sit in silence and observe my thoughts. I gradually still my mind by remembering that I am the master of the self and that I can choose my thoughts. I re-direct my thoughts towards my inner qualities. I remind myself that the things I do not like about myself are not part of my original nature, but are a result of suppressing the original nature of the self. I allow myself to become aware of the qualities I have inside. I now become aware of the love and peace that is within the self that does not depend on anything external to me. Let circumstances change, let people change, but let my value and love for myself remain constant. I am a soul, filled with love, peace, happiness, wisdom and strength.

As self-love is developed, violence will be replaced by non-violence and respect in all aspects of behaviour.

Violence Towards Others

The bridge between our state of being and violent behaviour towards others is attitude. Violence towards others comes from attitudes created by self-violence.

- Criticism
- Jealousy
- The desire to prove oneself
- The desire for recognition and respect
- Need to control others
- Exploitation
- Selfishness
- Impatience
- Dishonesty

A build-up of such attitudes within the family, workplace, community, between nations and towards the environment, leads to a global culture of disrespect.

Think of a person who you feel does not respect you. Pay special attention to showing that person respect and see how this changes your relationship with him/her.

Non-Violence

If lack of respect is an inherent aspect of violence, then non-violence is fostered through the cultivation of total respect for the self, others and the environment around us. Attitudes of non-violence foster such respect. These include

- A vision of equality – all are souls, children of One God, even though the costume of the body may vary in appearance from individual to individual.
- Generosity
- Love
- Listening
- Joy at the progress and success of others
- Patience
- Honesty

Non-Violent Lifestyle

To develop respect on an individual and global level, an attitude of trusteeship is necessary. All that we have has been given to us by God, in trust. Accordingly, we should use everything in alignment with God's wishes. If we use anything that we have with selfish motives, it will ultimately bring unhappiness. To be a trustee is to be honest and have a clear conscience, which results in inner peace and happiness.

The Bodhisattva of Compassion

All beings tremble before danger,
All fear death.
When a wo/man considers this,
S/he does not kill or cause to kill.

The Budda

Japanese Painting

Clouds of mosquitoes
It would be bare
Without them.

Issa

A BUDDHIST VIEW OF COMMITMENT TO A CULTURE OF NON-VIOLENCE AND RESPECT FOR LIFE

In Buddhism, not to kill is the first precept. It does not just mean not to kill ourselves or other people, it also means not to kill anything that is alive. When one practises Buddhism, one becomes aware of the preciousness of life and that all life is connected. Nobody wants to die. But it is also true to say that at some point in time everything dies. There is no escape. It could be tomorrow. It could be in fifty years time.

Who do you know with a short life-span? Who do you know who has lived or is living a long life?

Our life rests only upon one single breath. Life is precious because it might stop at any moment. To respect life, we have to appreciate its true value. We have to realise that there is a precarious life not only in me but also in all that lives. Not only in what is big and obvious but also in what is small and insignificant. In a way, a mosquito has as much right to live as an elephant, a baby as a murderer, a flower as a weed.

How sudden can death be?

In Buddhism, it is considered important to realise that we are equal in life, in the fact that we are born and that we all are breathing. We are different in our conditions, in our aspects, in our forms, in our qualities, in our abilities. But we are equal in the fact that we were born and that we are going to die, that we experience pain and that we can experience happiness. What is this life that we emerge into? How did it come about?

What is sustaining our life?

We depend upon all the conditions that form us: our parents, the food we eat, the air we breathe, the earth we walk upon, the clothes we wear, the water we drink, the house we live in, the friends we have, the society we partake in, the body/mind we have, etc.

Where and how does anything we use come to us?

When we have toast for breakfast, what is this piece of bread? Where does it come from? It started with the earth and some grains of wheat, sun and rain and human effort was added. A lot of energy was used to transform the grain into flour then into bread, then to bring it to our house. Are we aware of all the lives which have participated in the making of this piece of bread? When

In the same way as the hands and
so forth,
Are regarded as limbs of the body,
Likewise why are embodied
creatures
Not regarded as limbs of life?

I should dispel the misery of
others
Because it is suffering just like my
own,
And I should benefit others
Because they are living things, just
like myself.

Shantideva

Japanese monks gardening.

we eat this piece of toast, can we appreciate the lives and
energy involved in the making of it and respect them all,
yourself included who is eating the bread.

In Buddhism, there is the idea of interdependence, the
experience that everything depends on everything else.
Nothing exists separately from anything else. All that
lives, all that exists is connected. Realising this we cannot
but have compassion and respect for everything that is
alive.

So we have respect for life because we are an intrinsic
part of life. This respect for life not only requires us to
restrain from killing any life but also to protect it and care
for it, helping it to develop. This will ask us to reflect on
our impact on life, on our consumption, on our needs,
on our wants.

**How are we connected to the web of life? What do
we depend upon for living?**

What are our basic requirements?

What could be superfluous?

What is our positive/negative impact on life?

*Think of one living thing in your life other than a human
being, e.g. a tree or a cloud or a fish, and consider how it
is connected to you.*

You shall not kill!
Exodus 20:13 Jerusalem Bible

or

You shall not murder
Exodus 20:13 Revised Standard Version

It is the New Testament witness that God's answer to evil in this world lies in the cross.
John Ferguson, *The Politics of Love*,

To be sure, [Jesus] did not say that one should practise loving non-violence because it would always instantly transform enemies into bosom friends. The cross stands as a harsh reminder that love for enemies does not always work – at least in the short run.
Ron Sider *Christ and Violence*

It is God's nature never to do violence to any one

You leave the Spirit the moment you take up the cause of force instead of love ...

No one who has heard the clear call of Jesus' Spirit can resort to violence for protection. Jesus abandoned every privilege and every defence. He took the lowliest path.

He who is executed on the Cross can never execute anyone ...

He never kills; He Himself is killed.

He never crucifies; He Himself is crucified.

Eberhard Arnold, Hutterian Society of Brothers

A CHRISTIAN VIEW OF COMMITMENT TO A CULTURE OF NON-VIOLENCE AND RESPECT FOR LIFE.

Christianity has historically had three traditions on war: non-violence, just war and crusade.

Non-Violence

On the night of Jesus' arrest there were disciples with swords willing to fight for him. One did, drawing his sword and striking the slave of the high priest, cutting off his ear. Jesus said:

> Put your sword back into its place; for all who take the sword will perish by the sword. Do you think that I cannot appeal to my Father, and he will at once send to me more than twelve legions of angels. (Matthew 26: 52-53)

Tertullian an early Christian who lived 160-222 CE wrote the following response to this incident:

> For although soldiers had come to John and received the form of their rule, although even a centurion believed, the Lord afterwards in disarming Peter, disarmed every soldier. (*On Idolatry*)

For early Christians this was a decisive moment in the life of Jesus. Twelve legions of angels in today's terms is 36-72,000 paratroopers – quite a fighting force at Jesus' disposal! The crucifixion the next day is the culmination of Jesus' teaching and life. The cross is both God's argument against violence and God's commitment to life. It is irrefutable evidence that God loves his enemies.

For the first three hundred years no early Christian leader justified force or Christians serving in the army. Tertullian's stand was the norm, not the exception. Christianity at this time was a pacifist religious movement that endured periodically severe persecutions. It was a religion that suffered martyrdom but did not seek to make martyrs of others. The monastic tradition, the Mennonites, Amish and Hutterites along with the Quakers are examples of continuing Christian traditions that have remained committed to non-violence.

Just War and Crusade

Just War

Things changed when the Roman Emperor Constantine came to power in 312 CE. He ended the persecution of Christians and in his reign began the process of granting Christians privileges. Within a century if you were not a Christian you were persecuted in the Roman Empire. From this point on the Just War theory became the dominant teaching of the Christian church beginning with Augustine (354–430). The first systematic account appears in the *Decretum* of Gratian (c.1140). Just war thinking was further clarified in the sixteenth century by Catholic theologians De Vitoria (1483–1546) and Suarez (1548–1617). Both were concerned about the treatment of American Indians by Spanish kings in their conquest of what became Latin America. After the Protestant Reformation Just War teaching became part of the traditions of the Lutherans, Church of England, and the Presbyterian Church. Today the Just War theory remains the majority Christian position on war.

There are many versions of the criteria that justify war for Christians. One example is as follows:

a) **jus ad bellum 'the right to fight'**
- the authority waging war must be legitimate
- the cause being fought for must be just
- the motivation (intention) must be loving
- war must be the last resort
- success must be probable

b) **jus in bello 'fighting right i.e. fighting ethically'**
- the means must be indispensable
- the means must be discriminating (eg civilians cannot be the main target)
- the means must respect the provisions of international law[1].

Perhaps one of the best examples of justified violence was on the part of the German theologian and pastor, Dietrich Bonhoeffer, who played a part in the assassination attempt on Hitler in 1944. The weakness of this position is that Christian nations have slaughtered each other through European history whilst each side claimed it was a just war.

1. J.H.Yoder, *When War is Unjust*, pp.2-3

Martin Luther King in prison with Ralph Abernathy in 1964.
© United Press International and Holt, Rinehart and Winston, Inc, New York.

Crusade

In addition to Pacifism and Just War there is a third Christian position on war – Holy War or Crusade. In a Holy War or Crusade the unbeliever has no rights when God commands destruction. It is then legitimate to wipe out every man, woman and child and to burn their cities. In the twentieth century there have been secular crusades eg against Communism, Fascism and Capitalism. The Crusade is a discredited Christian position, a shameful chapter in Christian history. Yet nuclear weapons in their indiscriminate destructiveness could be argued to be weapons of crusade.

Non-Violent Resistance

Martin Luther King, influenced by Gandhi, perhaps developed a fourth Christian position – that of non-violent resistance – a position between Pacifism and Just War. The criteria for *jus ad bellum* the right to fight remain the same but *jus in bello* 'fighting right' can only ever be non-violent.

In summary, in the search for a non-violent global ethic Christians need critically to review their traditions on war and peace. The crusade is completely discredited. Although Just War criteria have been misused can this tradition, if given more rigour and objectivity, be an important tool in reducing violence? Or should Christians return to the pacificism of the early church? Finally, are the methods pioneered by Gandhi and Martin Luther King more faithful to the example of Jesus in non-violently resisting injustice?

Ideas for exploration:

1. The sixth commandment states 'You shall not kill!' (Exodus 20:13 RSV). Does this include killing in war?

2. Pacifism, Just War, Crusade or Non-Violent resistance – which position is closest to the example of Jesus?

3. Has there ever really been a just war?

4. Are Just War criteria valid in a nuclear age?

5. What Christian doctrine of war could be used to justify the violence between Catholics and Protestants in Northern Ireland?

A HINDU VIEW OF COMMITMENT TO A CULTURE OF NON-VIOLENCE AND RESPECT FOR LIFE

Mahatma Gandhi

May there be peace in the higher regions; may there be peace in the firmament; may there be peace on earth. May the waters flow peacefully; may the herbs and plants grow peacefully; may all the living powers bring unto us peace. The supreme Lord is peace. May we all be in peace, peace and only peace; and may that peace come unto each of us. Shanti, shanti, shanti.

Vedas

The mode of living which is founded upon a total harmlessness toward all creatures or (in case of actual necessity) upon a minimum of such harm, is the highest morality

Mahabharata, Shanti Parva 262,5-6

Respect for life is an ethical fundamental which Hinduism as a whole underwrites, but not absolutely. Similarly, non-violence is a well-known ideal and a principle which appeals to Hindus and which is followed in many sectarian groupings. Jainism, in particular, emphasises the ideal and basic principle of non-violence (*ahimsa*), to the extent that pious people will not eat lots of food items which other people consider perfectly innocent.

Respect for life and non-violence are high ideals, moral targets to aim for, rather than an ethical absolute. They operate within the ambit of *dharma*, the Hindu concept of macrocosmic and microcosmic order. Thus, violent means to terminate an aggressor's life are not only permitted in Hinduism, in fact they may be required in certain situations to uphold universal order. There is, then, no absolute prohibition on killing another human being, as a key passage in the famous epic poem of the Bhagavadgita shows.

Arjuna, who has particular doubts about whether it is all right to kill his close relatives on the other side in battle, is clearly told to 'go ahead and do it' because that is his duty in that situation. This shows us that Hinduism places respect for an individual life below the needs of society and the whole cosmic order. This does not justify indiscriminate killing, however, it only allows for the termination of those humans who positively obstruct and endanger a just, humane order of life. Obviously this can be abused in politics and in violent power struggles. It is not always easy to find out who is ultimately right, and who is wrong. But wrongdoers can be reminded that they are doing something wrong, and if they do not listen to reason and create disorder, more violent means are well within Hindu ideas about maintaining harmony and order.

When it comes to animal life, too, Hinduism takes a cautiously realistic view. It is the *dharma* of many animals to be eaten. Many Hindus eat meat, they may reflect on this before the meal, but most people probably ignore the fact that to prepare their food, an animal had to give its life. Carnivores among the animals would have real problems with this principle, but their way out is to argue that they should not kill senselessly and for pleasure, just to satisfy their hunger. Thus, a good Hindu lion just kills to eat!

44

Without doing injury to living beings, meat cannot be had anywhere; and the killing of living beings is not conducive to heaven; hence eating of meat should be avoided.

Manu Smriti 5,48

Happy the warriors indeed who become involved in such a war as this, presented by pure chance and opening the doors of paradise.

But if you will not wage this war prescribed by [your caste-]duty, then by casting off both duty and honour, you will bring evil on yourself.

Bhagavadgita 2, 32-33

Gandhi saw in *ahimsa* a positive moral force, which he called *satyagraha* or true-force

I . . . justify entire non-violence, and consider it possible in relations between man and man and nations and nations; but it is not 'a resignation from all real fighting against wickedness'. On the contrary, the non-violence of my conception is a more active and more real fighting against wickedness than retaliation whose very nature is to increase wickedness. I contemplate a mental, and therefore a moral opposition to immoralities. (*Non-violence in Peace and War* 1.44)

In daily life, Hindu respect for life and non-violence becomes apparent in many ways. Many Hindus are vegetarian or will only eat certain types of meat. A special cultural place is given to the cow, and eating beef is widely thought to be totally prohibited among Hindus. However, in some parts of South India, for example, this prohibition against eating beef is not maintained. Elsewhere, Hindus tell themselves that eating beefburgers is not a sin, so there are many ways round general prohibitions.

Strict vegetarians, on the other hand, will not even eat any living plants and may restrict their diet to dried substances, milk and water. This still causes problems if one remembers that dried nuts, for example, contain the source of life, as does every grain of rice or wheat. This example shows clearly that ideal concepts and human reality may not match well, so that a compromise has to be found.

A total prohibition on the killing of any life form can lead to grave health problems if, for example, rats are being worshipped and fed rather than destroyed, or if mosquitoes are allowed to breed and nobody bothers - or dares - to kill them. In some British cities, Hindus have been starting to feed pigeons, which has led to conflicts with local authorities over health concerns. The same issues arise in India and elsewhere.

'Gandhi claimed that the fight of which Krishna speaks in *The Gita* was a spiritual battle, and that the battlefield lay inside Arjuna. He said of *The Gita* that under the guise of physical warfare it described the duel that perpetually went on in the hearts of mankind, and that physical warfare was brought in merely to make the description of the internal duel more alluring. He used to assert that the central teaching of *The Gita* was selfless action (*anasakti*).. . . but Gandhi's exclusive emphasis on it is not the natural interpretation.' (From John Ferguson *War and Peace in the World's Religions* pp. 38–9)

Questions

Why do you think the Bhagavadgita was Gandhi's favourite text?

Do you think there are circumstances when it would be right to try to assassinate a tyrant?

A JAIN VIEW OF COMMITMENT TO A CULTURE OF NON-VIOLENCE AND RESPECT FOR LIFE

Jainism is one of the most ancient of Indian religious traditions. It is also the oldest non-Vedic school of thought. The word 'Jaina' is taken from 'Jina' which means conquerors or victors. Those who destroy all the bad karmas through austerities, penance and complete adherence to ahimsa become **arhats**. Jainas are the followers of Jinas - the twenty four Tirthankaras. The first Tirthankara was Lord Vrishabha and the last Tirthankara was Lord Mahavira (500 years BC). The Jain view of non-violence enjoins its followers to refrain from indulging in violence in thought, word and action. It believes in the equality of all living beings and in the state of equanimity. Ahimsa results from the equanimous state of mind. Ahimsa in the Jain tradition means reverence for all forms of life and avoidance of violence in thought, word and deed. A Jain ascetic observes ahimsa in its totality himself. He does not encourage others to resort to violence in thought, word and deed nor does he endorse it in thought, word and deed.

Ahimsa

Ahimsa is the highest point of the development of human civilization and culture. Himsa (violence) is inextricably intertwined with human life but is not considered a part of its development. More and more people in the world now realize the importance of ahimsa for human survival in the wake of the two nuclear holocausts that took the toll of two million lives in the forties of this century and the phenomenal rise of violence in the form of ethnic, religious and political wars and conflicts dotting the length and breadth of the globe today. Humanity seems to be heading fast for disaster. The incidents of ghastly violence that we witness in everyday life today cast a dark shadow over the future of humanity.

Violence: Definition and Causes

Before we analyze the causes of violence, let us first try to understand what we actually mean by violence. Some examples of physical violence have been given in the preceding paragraph but these examples describe just one aspect of violence. The noted Jain scholar Umasvati has defined violence in Tattvarth Sutra in the following words:

A Jain monk covers his mouth to avoid unintentionally taking life by swallowing an insect and sweeps the path to avoid stepping on any living creature. ©Ann and Bury Peerless, Birchington, Kent.

Injurious activities inspired by self-interest lead to evil and darkness. This is what is called bondage, delusion, death, and hell. To do harm to others is to do harm to oneself. 'Thou art he whom thou intendest to kill ! Thou art he whom thou intendest to tyrranize over !' We corrupt ourselves as soon as we intend to corrupt others. We kill ourselves as soon as we intend to kill others. (*Acaranga Sutra*)

46

'Taking life away out of passion is violence'

Passion includes the powerful emotions of anger, pride, deceit and greed or we can say that an injury to life motivated by passion is violence. If an injury is caused out of passion without deliberate intention, it does not of itself constitute an evil act since it is not accompanied by any feeling of attachment or hatred. As social beings we cannot escape violence in its totality so the Jain scriptures advise their votaries at least to refrain from unnecessary violence and follow ANUVRAT (basic vows). The acts of violence that we see in society today are being committed out of intense feelings of hatred, possessiveness and jealousy. Violence first arises in thought and is poured out verbally, in words. When passion grows uncontrollable, it leads to ghastly physical violence. Hence whether it is the unrestrained use of water, air, plants, vegetables or the unrestrained destruction of forests to satisfy one's limitless greed, the origin is the mind of man.

All religious traditions of the world agree that ahimsa alone can be the basis of our survival.

With the advent of Gandhi and Martin Luther King, the people in the West came to know of the word 'ahimsa', the nearest equivalent of which they found in their language was nonviolence. Ahimsa sprouts from a person's inner awakening. It conveys many things simultaneously whereas the word 'nonviolence' only indicates abstinence from physical violence.

The rapid ecological and environmental degradation witnessed in the last three decades of this century and the alarming trend of incidents of bloody feuds, arson, rape, looting and cruelty plunging humanity into chaos and anarchy have once again made ahimsa a global focus.

Gandhi and Ahimsa

Gandhi's legacy of ahimsa has created a deep impact on the world. He demonstrated to us the immense power of ahimsa by using it as an effective weapon to achieve independence for India without shedding blood. He was deeply influenced by the Jain scholar Raichandbhai. Gandhi has written, 'For me there is no religion other than the religion of truth, no duty other than ahimsa. Ahimsa is the greatest religion for me. I can say with assurance, as a result of my experiments, that a perfect vision of truth can follow a complete realization.'

Question

Can you think of a better translation for ahimsa than 'non-violence'?

A JEWISH VIEW OF COMMITMENT TO A CULTURE OF NON-VIOLENCE AND RESPECT FOR LIFE

Ethics of the Fathers:

'The world rests on three things, on truth on justice and on peace.'

Interpretation of the book of Numbers:

Great is peace, for even the angels in heaven need peace, as it says 'The Eternal makes peace in the high places'. Now can we not reason from the less important to the more important? If peace is necessary in heaven, a place where there is no hatred or enmity, how much more so is it necessary on earth, where so many conflicts are found.

Micah 4:2-5

Many nations will come and say,

'Come, let us go up to the mountain of the Eternal,

to the house of the God of Jacob.

God will teach us divine ways,

so that we may walk in his paths.

The law will go out from Zion

the word of the Eternal from Jerusalem.

God will judge between many peoples and will settle disputes for strong nations far and wide.

They will beat their swords into ploughshares and their spears into pruning hooks.

Nation will not take up sword against nation,

nor will they train for war any more.

Jewish tradition teaches that if someone is killed then a whole world is destroyed because not only that individual dies, but also all their potential descendants.

'Do not murder' is one of the most important religious commandments. But it is different from 'Do not kill'. In the Bible it was recognised that sometimes one person kills another without actually intending to do so – if they throw something without realising there was anyone there who could be hurt by it for instance. Someone who kills in this way is punished, but not as harshly as someone who deliberately set out to murder another person. This distinction between murder and manslaughter exists in modern law as well.

Self-defence is permitted and does not rate as murder if there is no other way to protect yourself. Traditional Jewish law distinguishes between wars which one must fight, where the country is being attacked and self-defence is necessary, and wars to gain more territory when soldiers are not obliged to fight.

If you see someone pursuing someone else, clearly intending to kill them when they catch them, then it is permitted to kill the one who is about to murder to save the life of their victim, although if it is possible to prevent them from killing by disabling them, rather than killing them, then that is preferable.

This law permitting the killing of the murderous pursuer is used to permit abortion when the pregnancy is putting either the mother's physical or mental health at serious risk.

Does killing animals count as murder? In the garden of Eden God told Adam and Eve to rule over the animals but not to eat them. Later in the Bible meat-eating was permitted. Jewish vegetarians now say that they are keeping the original perfect diet. Many other Jews say that eating meat adds to the joy of festive occasions and is permitted. It is still necessary to respect the creatures who die to give us pleasure. There is an ancient story about a rabbi towards whom a calf ran and hid, lowing in distress, on its way to be slaughtered. The rabbi pushed it away and said, 'Go, for it is for this that you were created'. He then suffered from several years misfortune to punish him for this heartless remark. His misfortunes only ended when he showed kindness to some weasels. While treating animals with kindness is

Everyone will sit under their own vine and under his own fig-tree, and no-one will make them afraid, for the Eternal Almighty has spoken.

All the nations may walk in the name of their gods, we will walk in the name of the Eternal our God for ever and ever.

Prayer for International Understanding

God of peace, be with those who guide the destinies of the world so that an end may come to boasting and vainglory, and the reign of arrogance dwindle in our time. Give them the courage to speak the truth and the humility to listen. Help us all to put the good of our fellow human beings above our own ambitions, and the truth which does not profit us above the lie which does. So may we stand upright, freed from the burden of fear and the weight of suspicion, learning to trust each other.

Help each one of us to bring our own offering of understanding, and our own sacrifice for peace, so that we are at peace with ourselves and live in peace with those around us. Then in tranquillity may we all go forward to build Your kingdom in the world until the earth shall be filled with Your knowledge as the waters cover the sea. Amen.

Forms of Prayer for Jewish Worship I, p. 297

important in Jewish teaching, animal life is never to be equated in value with human life.

The importance of taking care of the world and maintaining different species can be seen in these traditional interpretations of the Bible:

> In the hour when the Holy One created the first human being, God took the person before all the trees of the garden of Eden, and said to the person, 'See My works, how fine and excellent they are. All that I created, I created for you. Think upon this, and do not desolate and corrupt my world, for if you corrupt it, there is no one to set it right after you.'

(Interpretation of the Book of Ecclesiastes)

> 'Whatever God created has value'. Even the animals and the insects that seem useless and noxious at first sight have a vocation to fulfil. The snail trailing a moist streak after it as it crawls, and so using up its vitality, serves as a remedy for boils. The sting of a hornet is healed by the house-fly crushed and applied to the wound. The gnat, feeble creature, taking in food, but never secreting it, is a specific against the poison of a viper, and this venomous reptile itself cures eruptions, while the lizard is the antidote to the scorpion.

(Talmud Shabbat)

Peace is seen as something to long for and which is essential for the world in Jewish teaching.

Questions:

1. Is non-violence always compatible with respect for human life or are there circumstances where killing is justified?

2. Why is it important to distinguish between murder and manslaughter? Do you think this distinction is valid?

3. Why is human life more important than animal life?

4. What makes us responsible guardians of the world?

5. Should abortion be permitted?

A MUSLIM VIEW OF COMMITMENT TO A CULTURE OF NON-VIOLENCE AND RESPECT FOR LIFE

If they (your enemies) incline to peace incline thou to it as well, and place thy trust in God; verily, He alone is all-hearing, all knowing.

Qur'an 8:61

We ordained
For the children of Israel
That if anyone slew
A person - unless it be
for murder or for spreading
Mischief in the land -
It would be as if
He slew the whole people
And if anyone saved a life,
It would be as if he
Saved the life of the whole people

Qur'an 5.35

If one knows the true meaning of Islam, there will be no wars. All that will be heard are the sounds of prayer and the greetings of peace. Only the resonance of God will be heard. That is the ocean of Islam. That is unity. That is our wealth and our true weapon. Not the sword in your hand.

Sufi Shaikh M.R.Bawa Muhaiyaddeen, quoted in Living Religions, p.294

According to Abu Hurairah, the Messenger of God said, 'A man travelling along a road felt extremely thirsty and went down a well and drank. When he came up he saw a dog panting with thirst and licking the moist earth. "This animal", the man said, "is suffering from thirst just as much as I was" So he went down the well again, filled his shoe with water, and taking it in his teeth climbed out of the well and gave the water to the dog. God was pleased with his act and granted him pardon for his sins.'

The message of the Qur'an outlines our responsibilities to each other as members of families, communities and the human race. It outlines also our duties as stewards of the planet to safeguard its major features and the other living beings, animal and plants who share it with us. The Qur'an makes it clear that we are the vice-regents or trustees of this earth and therefore should keep our trust in the best way possible. Acts of violence would constitute a breach of this trust as it leads to damaging what we are supposed to improve or at least keep intact. Human history records our failures over the centuries to live up to our status as God's vice-regents. The present era is no worse than times past except in our current capacity to inflict greater damage through modern technology. Atrocities now claim more numerous victims than in previous times. This does not mean that humanity has slid down the ethical scale. It simply indicates that those dark forces in our psyche are now able through the use of weapons of mass destruction to inflict untold damage on large areas turning them into monuments of cruelty and savagery, annihilating all its living beings, natural resources and flora and fauna. Violence has thus grown in scale to such a degree that human society can no longer tolerate it. One of the blessings of modern technology is that the news of calamities befalling any part of the globe are broadcast world-wide. This should arouse opposition to those originated by human action. No amount of provocation can justify inflicting injury on others. The Qur'an tells us 'But (since) good and evil cannot be equal repel (evil) with something that is better. And lo! he between whom and thyself was enmity may then become as though he had always been (unto thee) a close friend' (*Surah 41 v.34.*)

This call to non-violence is further supported by the statement of the Prophet to his Companions that if two men fought each other and one was killed then both would go to hell. When the Companions asked in astonishment, saying that they understood why the murderer should be so punished but not why the murdered, he replied because the murdered wished to murder his opponent. The mere desire to commit an act of violence has thus been regarded as equal to the act itself. This is a clear and unambiguous call to Muslims to purge themselves of aggressive behaviour and embrace the culture of non-violence. But it is not enough to refrain from inflicting harm on other living beings. We

Someone said 'O Messenger of God, will we then have a reward for the good done to our animals?' 'There will be a reward'. he replied, 'for anyone who gives water to a being that has a tender heart.'

Hadith of Bukhart

Never does a Muslim plant trees or cultivate land, and birds or men or beasts eat out of them, but that is a charity on his behalf.

Hadith of Muslim

Jihad, 'striving in the cause of God', is usually translated as 'holy war', but this is misleading. Jihad is divided into two categories, the greater and the lesser; the greater jihad is the warfare in oneself against any evil or temptation. The lesser jihad is the defence of Islam, or of a Muslim country or community, against aggression. It may be a jihad of the pen or of the tongue. If it involves conflict, it is strictly regulated, and can only be defensive. Thus Muhammad said:

In avenging injuries inflicted on us, do not harm non-belligerents in their homes, spare the weakness of women, do not injure infants at the breast, nor those who are sick. Do not destroy the houses of those who offer no resistance and do not destroy their means of subsistence, neither their fruit trees, nor their palms.

Jihad cannot be undertaken to convert others because there 'cannot be compulsion in religion' (*Qur'an* 2.256). If these regulations seem on occasion to be ignored, that failure is an offence to be answered for on the Day of Judgement

The Oxford Dictionary of World Religions. Ed. John Bowker

must, as Islam instructs us, do our utmost to prevent harm from falling upon others whether the source is an act of God or the act of a human being.

Opposition to violence from whatever source and extending help to the victim regardless of identity pervades the ethical teaching of Islam. We are daily bombarded with news about disasters, earthquakes, drought, civil strife and war. Our responsibilities are to help the victims of the Acts of God and use all means possible to ward off human aggression. The Qur'an declared that God does not like aggressors. The Prophet set an example of how to act when others face a calamity. His enemies in Makkah, those who killed and tortured his followers and who plotted to assassinate him, suffered a severe drought and faced starvation. They sent him a message asking for help. Some of his Companions advised that the enemies should be allowed to die of hunger, but the prophet ordered grain to be sent to them although he was well aware not only of their past misdeeds but also of their certain future acts of violence against Muslims. He regarded the saving of life in such circumstances as an absolute moral principle which should not be compromised by practical considerations.

Islam defines violence to include all forms of aggressive behaviour whether by gesture, words or deeds. As we know, violence takes many forms ranging from physical and verbal abuse and should be resisted, by fighting if necessary, both on our own and on other's behalf. Modern warfare is contrary to our rules of war in my opinion. As already stated, war can sometimes be a necessary evil. Islam decrees it must be for upholding justice and its rules of engagement must avoid harming non-combatants as well as the environment. Muslim commanders are directed to respect places of worship, peaceful priests and nuns, water supplies, orchards and other major assets.

We often face disagreements which escalate into fierce arguments and even the breaking of friendship. Such things as football matches, which television programme to watch or where to go on holiday can lead to enmity. We are advised to listen to an arbiter respected by both sides.

Question

Do you think economic sanctions which can cause starvation and illness should be used against nations that engage in aggression?

What is the best way of resolving a sharp disagreement in a family?

A RASTAFARIAN VIEW OF COMMITMENT TO A CULTURE OF NON-VIOLENCE AND RESPECT FOR LIFE

There will be mourning and weeping for her by the kings of the earth who have fornicated with her and lived with her in luxury. They see the smoke as she burns, while they keep at a safe distance from fear of her agony. They will say: 'Mourn, mourn for this great city, Babylon, so powerful a city, doomed as you are within a single hour' (Rev.18:v.9-10

The Rastafarian God is a 'God of Redemption', redeeming the African people from injustice, brutality, exploitation and colonial domination. There is an express duty to fight injustice and oppression. In the words of His Imperial Majesty Emperor Haile Selassie I (immortalised by Bob Marley in the song 'War') in respect of racial injustice in Africa: 'We Africans will fight if necessary, because we are confident in the victory of good over evil.' The same God that gave the command 'Thou shalt not kill' did not hesitate to wipe out entire communities (men, women, children, animals and possessions) when they had fallen into the abyss of wickedness.

The book of Revelation is in essence a forecast of the world wide destruction of the wicked and eternal life for those who live according to his dictates. The reference in the Book of Revelations to Babylon is for most Rastafarians a reference to nations of the West, and their imminent destruction by Jah is a foregone conclusion. Accordingly, many Rastafarians pray for the destruction of the wicked world of 'Men' and strive to 'leave Babylon' (the West) by repatriation to Mother Africa. However, the Rastafarian commitment to peace and love ensures that Rastafarians, even the most militant, are originally the most peaceful and long suffering people on this planet. As pointed out by the Hon. Marcus Mosiah Garvey, the foremost Rastafarian prophet, 'God is a bold sovereign – A Warrior Lord'. The God we worship and adore is a God of War as well as a God of Peace. He does not let anything interfere with his power and authority.' For many Rastas those same principles demonstrated by Jah are applicable to humanity.

Many Rastas have quite eloquently demanded respect and recognition, based on the bedrock of love, charity, equity and justice (not the justice that makes distinctions between peoples and races, but the justice that is applied for its own sake).

The Hon. Marcus Mosiah Garvey mandated that upon such a foundation the African race should be built, ensuring the eternal blessings of our Creator and he asked 'who is to tell that we shall not teach men the way to life, liberty and true human happiness?'[1] The

---

[1] M. Garvey, *Philosophy and Opinions of Marcus Garvey* p.14.

Bap!! Sheebam!! Sheeboom!!

The spirit searching for
connections!

To see the world for what it is and
for what it can be. To tell truths
that show the blue mist rising, that
show the sun shining. To make the
old, courting despair, laugh. To
become the beggarman/chink in
the King's palace armour.

To see the causes. To see the effects.
To see the need for action. To be
unafraid of the quiet cold of death.
To fall. To rise to be cut down. To
rise again . . That the way sometimes cannot be but blood, is a
red/dripping truth that hangs in
the long night. A referent to our
dilemma: the dark quiet room . .
They try to stifle the spirit, they
cannot. They will try, but the spirit
pulls as the equinoxes pull and
plants the seeds in the souls of the
dead and in the wombs of the
unborn. The night is long and the
morning's light does not shine
unless you fight, fight, fight for it.

Rites for Walter Rodney, by Clifton
Joseph, *The Global Dilemma*

Rastafarian God is a God of love, charity, equity and
justice! This also imposes a duty on all Rastafarians to
defend the body (Temple of Jah) against external threats
of physical aggression. In this regard Rastas consider this
as adhering to the dictate of 'love' (for Jah is love),
respect for all living things and the defence of Mother
Africa to ensure a fullness of life. This means resorting
to self-defence by any means necessary, even if this
entails engaging in violent armed conflict. To fail to do
this is to fail in one's duty to protect and preserve the
'Temple of Jah' and is an insult to Jah.

The defence of the African people 'at home and abroad'
is also important to many Rastafarians. For many, it is an
'irrevocable directive' that the freedom of the African
people, whether on the Continent or in the diaspora,
must be defended and attained by any means necessary.
Hence in the world of Pan-African Rastafarian heroes
we find at the forefront those who resisted slavery, injustice and oppression through armed struggle. Sam
Sharpe, Paul Bogle, Nannie of the Maroons, Toussaint
L'Ouverture, Christophe, and Dessalines all stand out as
role models. They engaged in genuine armed liberation
struggles, which history demonstrates to be the only path
to freedom for many oppressed peoples.

As we have seen, concepts of peace and love are central
to Rasta doctrine. All of humanity's progress over the
past five hundred years has been a direct result of these
forces. However, on the other hand, if it were not for
oppression, racism and bloodshed, mankind would be
twenty times more advanced. This reality dictates that
Rastas follow the path of peace and love.

However, from an individual Rastafarian perspective,
peace and the permanent settlement of human ills can
never be attained by international conferences or grand
sounding declarations, but only by going to the root of
evil that one finds in racial injustice and prejudice. As
long as humanity is reduced to a world of second class
citizenship and first, second and third world realities, it
is inevitable that there will be wars. A failure to move
away from this path is to continue on the path of 'Men'
– which can only lead to ultimate destruction.

> ### Question
>
> 'That the way sometimes cannot be but blood is a
> red/dripping truth . . .'
>
> Do you agree that the demands of justice sometimes
> require violent action?

੧੬

A SIKH VIEW OF COMMITMENT TO A CULTURE OF NON-VIOLENCE AND RESPECT FOR LIFE

As the mother gives birth to a son, keeps a constant watch over him and brings him up.

At home and outside feeds him with nourishing food and loves him every moment.

In the same way, the true Guru Cares for his follower with deep love.

GGS-168

The age is knife

The kings are butchers

Religion has taken wings

and flown in the dark night of falsehood

The rise of the moon of truth

Is nowhere to be seen.

Guru Nanak: GGS-145

Those who beat you with fists, do not give them blows

Go to their homes yourself and kiss their feet.

Baba Farid : GGS-1378

If it is said that there is God in every being, why then kill a chicken?

Kabir : GGS-1350

In the Sikh tradition 'the right to life' is a sacred right and therefore must be respected. Life is given to us by God and is sacred. Therefore, it is not for us to take. As a child from God, every individual has the right to develop in safety to achieve his/her full potential. It is equally important to accept the rights of others. Adults have the duty to provide a safe and conducive environment for the nurture of the young and for the care of the weak and elderly. A mother brings up children without any expectation of reward or return.

This parental love is selfless, but to repay their care with arguments and disrespect is considered a sin.

To abandon one's parents even for worship or for reading the scriptures and for serving others is not acceptable. On the other hand, such action would hinder spiritual progress.

Similarly the state has the duty of care for its people. No state or nation has the right to subjugate people, to discriminate against sections of society, put on them burdensome taxation and not provide protection for people within their frontiers. Guru Nanak was scathing in his attack on rulers who were oppressing their people rather than safeguarding them, as can be seen in the verse in the first column.

He also made a comment about rulers as 'the fence eating away the crop it is meant to protect.' It is the moral, economic and social responsibility of those who are in charge to provide for the welfare of everybody.

According to the Sikh faith, we should all aim for a just and moral order. Without it there would always be conflict, given our human weaknesses. We should continue to work towards resolving conflict through peaceful methods. Taking up arms should not be the first resort. It is only used as a last resort. Guru Gobind Singh, the tenth Guru said in a letter to the Mughal Emperor:

Countless commit sin by behead-
ing

Japji Sahib, Verse 18

Air is the Guru, Water the father

Earth the great mother

Day and night are male and female
nurses,

In whose laps the whole world
plays.

Japji Sahib : GGS-8

Practical Concerns of the Sikhs

Many Sikhs come from farming
backgrounds, where they have
close association with animals and
nature. They support initiatives for
the protection, preservation and
care of the environment.

Sikhs believe that there are
8,400,000 life forms and the soul
may transmigrate to any of these.
The human form is rare and carries
with it responsibility towards
others. We are all interdependent
and need each other to survive.
Harmony with other parts of
nature is essential. In Japji Sahib,
which is recited by the Sikhs every
morning, this relationship with
nature is very deep and very close
as in the raising of the young in
the human family.

Therefore, concern for others and
readiness to help is an essential
part of the Sikh code of conduct,
both at an individual and at a
social level. Being a minority of
only 20 million world wide, and
having been subjected to persecution throughout their five hundred
year old history, they would wish
a world order in which all minorities, whether racial, ethnic, religious or linguistic or any other
type are protected.

'When all other means of resolving conflict and
obtaining justice fail then it is appropriate to wield the
sword'[1].

Now with nuclear weapons of various types, there can
be no survival for humanity without commitment to
resolving matters through non-violent means. There are
some Sikh groups who are committed to following the
total non-violent path for achieving solutions. They
follow the fifth and ninth Gurus who remained peaceful,
even when violence was inflicted on them, so much so
that they lost their lives.

The Sikh history from the middle of the nineteenth
century till 1984, has been one of non-violent struggle for
rights of religious and political autonomy. Many lost
their lives, but did not resort to arms. The Sikhs are
usually very co-operative and open. They abide by the
laws of the land, but if the laws are unfair, they would
work towards getting them changed through non-
violent means. They are generally willing to work within
the Sikh community and outside to help young people
to develop non-violent ways of settling differences and
to help build a culture of non-violence, wherever they
live in the world. Violence is a sin, which we should
shun.

Many Sikhs are vegetarian and no meat, fish or egg is
served in the Sikh place of worship. There are some Sikhs
who are non-vegetarian, but they do not eat beef or halal
meat.

Ideas for exploration

1. The Sikhs say they respect life. Find out by
   talking to a Sikh, how do they do it in practice.
   Do you need to be a vegetarian to respect life?

2. In the present day context, how do you apply
   the saying of Guru Nanak that 'the fence is
   eating the crop it is meant to protect.'

3. Why might a Sikh take up a sword?

---

1. From *Zafarnama*, Guru Gobind Singh's Reply to Aurangzeb, c.1705

A ZOROASTRIAN VIEW OF COMMITMENT TO A CULTURE OF NON-VIOLENCE AND RESPECT FOR LIFE

Through good deeds and words and deep meditation O, Mazda, whereby the people will attain eternal life, righteousness, spiritual strength and perfection, I will dedicate them all to Thee, O Ahura, as a gift.

GY 34,1

The law and custom of Holy Khordod is fertility and prosperity. Keep your heart happy and keep your body pure, for purity of the body is the righteousness of the mind. Do not be ungrateful and do not be sad. Look upon the world with a positive eye and be grateful for the gifts and laws of Bountiful Ahura Mazda. Out of barrenness create fertility and produce happiness. Since water is the source of fertility and prosperity, keep water clean. Do not contaminate the water with impurity. Do not wash your body nor clothes in flowing water. Dig canals and turn dry land into productive land.

The law and custom of Holy Amordod is physical health and long life. Keep your bodies competent and in good condition. Keep distant from lies and contamination. Keep your homes and your clothes clean. Drain stagnant water and waterlogged land and in its place create cultivated land. Plant trees and plants. Do not cut down young trees. Do not harvest unripe fruit. Give herbs and medicines to the needy. Look after those who are ailing or in pain.

(Marriage Liturgy)

The followers of untruth try to prevent those who support Asha from advancing towards their sacred goal, i.e. truthfulness, righteousness and flourishing of the province and country. They are well-known for their unfriendly actions. The persons who oppose

A Zoroastrian is expected to respect all manifestations of the Creator on earth, be they fellow humans, other living creatures, the earth itself or the elements around it. This means that we should approach and treat each aspect with love, gentleness and kindness.

To arrive at this non-violent state of mind, we need to have peaceful minds which will also allow us to hear the voice of conscience which helps us to make reasoned judgements. To achieve an unclouded mental state, much emphasis is put on cultivation. It is believed that exercise and work in the outdoors while working in harmony with the earth, the water and the plants, is conducive to clarity of mind and inner peace. Of course this amounts to a form of meditation, since there is tranquility around which leads to contemplation of beauty and produces a sense of awe.

Cultivation also has the end result of food production and where food is plentiful, and land is in production, the need to fight over food resources is reduced and leads to harmonious co-existence with neighbours. Beyond this, the production of cereals, vegetables and fruit provides a balanced diet, which although unknown in Zoroaster's day, is now acknowledged as having an important part to play in reducing violence and aggression.

To be able to produce goods in excess of your needs is considered to be a desirable target since that allows you to give away some of the surplus to provide for the needy and less fortunate. In addition to the ability to be charitable, which is fundamental to Zoroastrian practice, by working hard and having more than you need, you are able to store away food for an occasion when a special event requires celebration, or disaster hits.

The stewardship of the earth and the non-pollution of the elements is a central duty, and a Zoroastrian hurts inside to see the violence perpetrated on the planet these days. The importance of keeping water supplies clear and useable, the earth clean and untainted, and the air around unsullied has always been taught to Zoroastrian children, but the significance of this teaching for the late twentieth century is only now becoming apparent as we confront environmental disasters daily.

Animals too have a particular place in Zoroastrian teaching and four days a month are put aside on which meat must not be consumed nor animals killed. In any the followers of untruth, O Mazda, with heart and soul, shall lead the world to real and true wisdom.

GY 46, 40

Armaiti, do not allow the tyrants and bad rulers rule over us, but let the good and just kings, guided by wisdom and good and clear understanding rule over us. Dedication to purity is best for man since his birth. We should toil for the Mother Earth and progress of the world, leading all the creatures on to the Light and the Truth.

She, Armaiti, is indeed our safe refuge. She brings the soul strength and life renewed, the true qualifications of the pure mind. Mazda Ahura has clothed Her, the Mother Earth, with vegetation, and has covered Her with food for people, since the dawn of life. Such is the wisdom of Mazda and the Eternal Law of Asha.

Keep hatred and anger far away from yourselves. Let nothing tempt you to violence. Hold on to love and good mind. Brilliant teachers, who wish to hold fast on to Truth, shall lead the followers of truth to paradise, Thy abode, O Ahura, where the righteous people dwell.

GY 48, 5-7

Let no one give ears to the words of false and the wicked ones, because such persons shall lead the home, the village, the town and the country to ruin and destruction. It is, therefore, our duty to resist such persons and repel them with spiritual weapons of purity and righteousness.

GY 31, 18

event, meat was traditionally a treat for special occasions and not consumed in the large quantities we are used to today, and before killing an animal, a prayer of acknowledgement and for forgiveness was recited. One day in the month known as the day of *Bahman* (derived from the older version *vohu manah* - **good mind**) is a day devoted to giving all animals a special day of rest and special treats like some different food, garlands etc.

In discussing a **fully human life,** the importance of freedom to choose the right path and to listen to the inner voice of conscience were mentioned. Since great importance is attached to each person's own choice of path, for this reason a Zoroastrian will not attempt to force anyone to accept or follow their particular philosophy, no matter how superior they may think it to be, nor how misguided the other's way of thinking. Using no force or violence to impose a theological, ethical or political order but hoping to convince merely by action and example is the Zoroastrian way to persuade.

Rulers are thought to have particular responsibilities and are exhorted to consider the best interests not of themselves but of their people. An enlightened leader with an acute conscience who commands respect by his/her enlightened government is the model laid down by Zoroaster. Many of the kings of ancient Iran (e.g. Cyrus the Great and Darius) were renowned for just rule and their tolerance of and respect to those of other faiths. In these ways and others, Zoroastrians are taught to have respect for life and to pursue a life of non-violence.

Questions

What food or drink is more likely to make you violent or aggressive?

What situations are liable to make you feel aggressive?

What do you think are the main causes of war?

SECTION C

C. 2

The Second Directive is:

Commitment to a culture of solidarity and a just economic order

A BAHA'I VIEW OF COMMITMENT TO A CULTURE OF SOLIDARITY AND A JUST ECONOMIC ORDER

The fundamentals of the whole economic condition are divine in nature and are associated with the world of the heart and spirit ... Hearts must be so cemented together, love must become so dominant that the rich shall most willingly extend assistance to the poor and take steps to establish these economic adjustments permanently. If it is accomplished in this way it will be most praise-worthy because then it will be for the sake of God and in the path-way of His service.

'Abdu'l-Baha, *Promulgation of Universal Peace* 233

Regarding economic prejudice, it is apparent that whenever the ties between nations become strength-ened and the exchange of com-modities accelerated, and any economic principle is established in one country, it will ultimately affect the other countries and universal benefits will result. Then why this prejudice?

'Abdu'l-Baha, *Baha'i Peace Pro-gramme* 15

This readjustment of the social economic order is of the greatest importance inasmuch as it ensures the stability of the world of humanity; and until it is effected, happiness and prosperity are impossible.

'Abdu'l-Baha, *Promulgation of Universal Peace* 176

The Baha'i Writings make frequent mention of 'true civilization', referring to a more ideal world-wide situation which must come in the future if this world is to progress.

Past models of governance are out-dated. In the fields of law, thought, and ethics we need new models to serve modern times. Think of the progress during the past century in arts and sciences, industry, and invention. In these areas it is clear that knowledge has progressed greatly. So too, in relation to the needs of the world, this must be a time of re-formation and renewal in the ways we approach problems.

Past models were designed to deal with localized and national situations, but in these times our view must be global, and this demands new solutions and methods.

The characteristics of a 'true civilization' are –

- it is global in its scope, and beyond prejudice;
- it is based on spiritual values which recognize justice for all of the world's citizens;
- its governing institutions are not motivated by considerations of personal gain.

True civilization will come into being through –

- the sincere will of leaders of nations to transform present unideal systems;
- committed effort by governments that will use their skill to put far-reaching reforms into action;
- the dedicated and determined effort of all people to bring about necessary change.

Necessary steps to establish 'true civilization' include –

- the promotion of education. The main reason for lack of progress in a nation is the ignorance of its people;
- The getting-together of groups of experts on subjects to do with law, order, and government, to act as advisors to governments;
- agreement by heads of nations to do all in their power to 'establish the Cause of Universal Peace', and make binding treaties to safeguard and promote its progress;
- making the above resolution known to all people.

A new religious principle is that prejudice and fanaticism whether sectarian, denominational, patriotic, or political are destructive to the foundation of human solidarity; therefore man should release himself from such bonds in order that the oneness of the world of humanity may become manifest.

'Abdu'l-Baha, *Promulgation of Universal Peace* 450

The remedy must be legislative readjustment of conditions. The rich too must be merciful to the poor, contributing from willing hearts to their needs without being forced or compelled to do so. The composure of the world will be assured by the establishment of this principle in the religious life of mankind.

'Abdu'l-Baha, *Promulgation of Universal Peace* 103

The primary, the most urgent requirement is the promotion of education. It is inconceivable that any nation should achieve prosperity and success unless this paramount, this fundamental concern is carried forward. The principal reason for the decline and fall of peoples is ignorance.

'Abdu'l-Baha, *Secret of Divine Civilization* 109

'Beyond prejudice' means that bias based on religious belief, nationality, or political views, should be abandoned, as such preferences destroy the very basis of the unity of humankind. This is a good example of the need for new models in this time. The Prophet Baha'u'llah has made the abolition of prejudice a new religious principle for the modern age.

Justice requires that existing inequalities are evened-out and that all citizens of the world receive a more just share of the earth's resources. This means all people, not only those favoured by being born in more developed nations or in better-off societies and families, have a right to enjoy a good standard of living. When standards are raised in any country, other nations will eventually benefit.

Education must be open and made readily available to all people. Everyone should be educated in a range of subjects - arts and sciences - so as to be able to work to improve their conditions. Education should be based on virtues and values so that the mass of the population base their actions on principles of justice for all rather than on merely what is to their own advancement and benefit.

Group discussion

Imagine you are members of a governing institution – for example, a school board, local council, national parliament. Select a relevant topical issue to discuss. Spend half the available discussion time debating the issue on the basis of usual present-day considerations and values. Then discuss the same issue considering wider values of justice, 'the good and happiness of all people', peace between nations, and lack of personal gain.

A BRAHMA KUMARIS VIEW OF COMMITMENT TO A CULTURE OF SOLIDARITY AND A JUST ECONOMIC ORDER

Simplicity, economy and self-sufficiency have been key values for the Brahma Kumaris since its inception. In 1936, Brahma Baba, the founder of the Brahma Kumaris World Spiritual University, left an affluent life as a diamond merchant, to dedicate his wealth to the creation of the University and adopt for himself a simple, spiritual lifestyle. Through his own example, he taught simplicity, economy and self-sufficiency. During the first fourteen years, the students lived together, milling their own flour, growing their own vegetables, making their own clothes and shoes and so on.

Working from the premise of 'when we change, the world changes', Brahma Baba encouraged efficient use of **all** resources – those which are physical as well as those belonging to the inner, spiritual realm. He believed that without the right use of spiritual resources, the right use of physical resources would not be possible. In the teachings that he shared, he described principles governing the use of spiritual resources.

Each one of us has many spiritual treasures within (such as our virtues and values), which we either waste or use well. Certain principles govern the right use of these spiritual treasures. They include:

- Use your spiritual wealth to serve many, not just your own self;

- The more you share your (spiritual) wealth with others, the more it will increase;

- The more you use your spiritual resources in an appropriate and effective way, the more powerful they become;

- Be generous hearted in using your resources for a worthy elevated purpose, but be sparing when it comes to anything unproductive. Let there be less expense, yet greater results.

From simplicity grows generosity. Generosity is sharing hard earned income with liberality of spirit. Sharing one's own resources in a congenial and caring manner is to bring back to human activity the meaning of family. Simplicity is more than giving money and material possessions. It is the giving of the self, which is price-less - patience, friendship and encouragement. In the spirit of putting others first, those embracing simplicity donate their time freely to others. That is done with kindness, openness, and pure intentions and without expectations and conditions. As a result, such individuals reap the abundant fruit sown from the seeds of generous actions. (Living Values)

The ethic of simplicity teaches economy. Simplicity is the conscience which calls upon people to rethink their values. Simplicity decreases the gap between 'the haves' and 'the have nots' by demonstrating the logic of true economics: to earn, save, invest, and share the sacrifices and the prosperity so that there can be a better quality of life for all people, regardless of where they were born. (Living Values)

A basic human need is to feel a sense of belonging, to be a part of a unified whole. People do not want to remain in isolation, oblivious to the world outside. It is also uniquely human to be curious about other people and cultures and to feel a deep sense of compassion over sufferings of and injustices done to others. It is, therefore, human instinct to want to be together and to form natural gatherings or structured meetings which provide a common platform to talk to each other. In such ways people get to know, understand or help each other. This holds true for individuals as well as nations. Consciously or unconsciously, we choose to act together. (Living Values)

It is important to understand and practice the correct use of physical resources if we wish to develop a just economic order. This is because the correct use of physical resources is a natural reflection of the accurate use of spiritual resources.

- *Time is very precious and therefore we often think that time should only be used for ourselves and for our own relaxation and enjoyment. Experiment with giving some of your time to helping others. Offer your time; do not wait to be asked. Afterwards, think about the effect this has had on your feelings and sense of well being.*

From Generosity to Economy

There is a strong link between the values of generosity, unity, simplicity and economy.

- The more you give, the more you receive;

- Unity leads to the sharing and efficient use of resources;

- A simple lifestyle economises on the use of resources.

How could you simplify your lifestyle? Do you waste any resources? Decide on one change today in your lifestyle.

Think about the effect this could have on you and the world around you.

A BUDDHIST VIEW OF COMMITMENT TO A CULTURE OF SOLIDARITY AND A JUST ECONOMIC ORDER.

The Five Precepts – are basic guides to living that all Buddhists observe:

To refrain from killing or harming living beings;

To refrain from taking what is not given;

To refrain from licentiousness and sexual misconduct;

To refrain from falsehood and all wrong speech;

To refrain from drink or drugs which dull the mind.

The Ten Perfections

Buddhists seek to develop the perfection of generosity, virtue, simplicity, wisdom, energy, forbearance, truthfulness, resolution, love, serenity.

The Buddha was always clear that the basic nature of everyone (buddha nature) is the same. He accepted those from every class, caste and background, even former criminals, into his spiritual Order. Buddhist monks shave their hair and wear a simple robe, so as to remove all distinctions of social superiority/inferiority. In the twentieth century, large numbers of Indians who lived below the caste system and were regarded as inferior have "taken refuge" in the Buddha because Buddhism accepts them completely as equal human beings.

There is a common misunderstanding that Buddhism teaches a rejection of the good things of life. This is untrue; what we are warned against is grasping and trying to hold onto the things that attract us. The Buddha taught that all suffering is caused by the Three Poisons; ignorance, hatred and greed. Because we forget our true nature, we imagine a separate self with its own desires. This causes endless frustration and conflict with others. Having lost touch with life, we feel always deprived and want endless "presents" to satisfy our empty feeling. The image for this is the "hungry ghost" with a big, empty belly and a tiny throat, always begging for more.

Getting more and more will definitely not make everyone happy. In fact, trying to satisfy all our desires is impossible (and could wreck the planet). The Buddha was careful to include "Right Livelihood" in the path that he recommended; getting what we need without hurting others. Working out the meaning of Right Livelihood is the biggest challenge facing the human race in the 21st century – and each one of us.

Thinking that you can buy your way out of society's problems is based on a delusion. Because we are all completely interdependent, we cannot afford to pursue individual solutions. The Dalai Lama (the head of Tibetan Buddhism) says that humanity's survival requires "universal responsibility"; seeing everyone's happiness as our business. He also says "my religion is kindness".

Advising people to live simply, with restraint, does not mean that it is acceptable for people to be poor and wretched. The Buddha had strong words with rulers of his day who neglected to help the poor. Poverty makes people desperate, he said, they will steal and resort to violence. Inequality creates suspicion and mistrust, an upward spiral of conflict, less respect for women,

The Boddhisattva Vows

A Boddhisattva is one who lives the awakened life for the benefit of all, taking these vows;

1. I vow to deliver innumerable sentient beings.

2. I vow to cut off endless vexations.

3. I vow to master limitless approaches to Dharma (Truth).

4. I vow to attain supreme Awakening.

children and elderly people. Does this sound like today's newspaper? The Buddha was talking 2,500 years ago, but he seems to have pointed to things which do not change.

In early times, the monks owned only a robe, a bowl and whatever food generous people put into it. But generous kings gave great wealth to the Order, so monks came to live in huge monasteries, temples and universities, where they could easily lose touch with ordinary people's sufferings. It was Buddhism for the professionals, focussed on the highest states of wisdom but perhaps lacking in day to day kindness. Forgetting that the Buddha taught liberation in this life, they tended to promise the poor rebirth in a paradise (or as monks), instead of working for justice. In India, Buddhism almost died out, perhaps because it lost the involvement of ordinary people.

In many countries today there is a challenge for the Buddhist Order; whether to support or to speak out against the powerful, the wealthy and the government, when they are corrupt and repressive. It is easy to keep quiet. On the other hand, there are those monks, nuns and lay people who spend their time working on social problems or trying to protect nature against greedy, destructive "development". Buddhism is most alive where it engages with suffering and the causes of suffering.

As Buddhism comes to Europe and America, it faces the same issues. Are Buddhist groups to become businesses, focussed on acquiring property and recruiting affluent professional people, while staying away from anything 'controversial'? Or will they share the life of those who are really suffering and who need the teaching of wisdom and compassion the most? Some people are making it their spiritual practice to help the dying, prisoners, addicts or the homeless.

Will getting what we want make us happy?

Is what we need different from what we think we want?

A CHRISTIAN VIEW OF COMMITMENT TO A CULTURE OF SOLIDARITY AND A JUST ECONOMIC ORDER

Clean water is made available to this North Indian village by Christian Aid.

You shall not steal

Exodus 20: 15

Everything should be common to all, as it is written, and no one should call anything his own or treat it as such.

The Rule of St Benedict

Whose side is God on – the rich or the poor? Consider the enslaved Hebrews in Egypt:

Then the Lord said, 'I have seen the affliction of my people who are in Egypt, and have heard their cry because of their taskmasters; I know their sufferings, and I have come down to deliver them out of the hand of the Egyptians, and to bring them up out of that land to a good and broad land, a land flowing with milk and honey' (Exodus 3:7-8)

God, in this famous story, is clearly on the side of the poor. After Exodus – the escape to freedom – the former Hebrew slaves received God's law at Mount Sinai. This has been called a second 'exodus' - a constitution for the people of Israel – that was meant to prevent the re-creation of the injustices of the Egyptian society that they had left. For example every seven years, the Sabbath year required the release of debts and slaves and the Jubilee year every fifty years required the return of land to its original owners to prevent the rich gaining too much control. The land was the Lord's and was for all, not just the prosperous. It could only be leased, not sold.

The prophetic tradition in the Jewish scriptures affirms time and again God's solidarity with the poor. For instance the prophet Isaiah spoke in warning to the people of Israel as follows:

> *cease to do evil,*
> *learn to do good;*
> *seek justice,*
> *correct oppression,*
> *defend the fatherless,*
> *plead for the widow.*
> *(Isaiah 1:17)*

At the beginning of Jesus' ministry it was from the scroll of Isaiah that he read the following in the Nazareth synagogue:

> *The Spirit of the Lord is upon me,*
> *because he has anointed me to*
> *preach good news to the poor.*
> *He has sent me to proclaim release to the captives*
> *and recovery of sight to the blind,*
> *to set at liberty those who are oppressed,*
> *to proclaim the acceptable year of*
> *the Lord.*
> *(Luke 4:18-19)*

If the sun were not hung up so high, it would long ago have been claimed by a few people as their private property, to the detriment of the rest who would then see nothing at all.

Old Hutterian saying

What is 'private'? What does 'private' mean? A private business, private car, private property, private road? *Privare* means to steal. Stolen property, then. Stolen from whom? From God and humankind, taken away from God's creation!

Eberhard Arnold

The social influence of the church is a fact. Not to exercise this influence in favour of the oppressed of Latin America is really to exercise it against them.

Gustavo Gutierrez *The Theology of Liberation*

This reading picks up the prophetic passion of justice for the poor. It has been suggested that this passage contains clear references to the Sabbatical and Jubilee Years. Some scholars have argued that Jesus was announcing permanent jubilee. The rich young ruler who questioned Jesus about what was required for eternal life was told 'One thing you lack. Sell all that you have and distribute to the poor, and you will have treasure in heaven; and come, follow me'. (Luke 18:22)

Luke in the book of Acts describes how the early Jerusalem Church from Pentecost lived as follows:

> And all who believed were together and had all things in common; and they sold their possessions and goods and distributed them to all, as any had need. (Acts 2:44-45)

The monastic tradition has continued this radical way of living with all things in common. So have the Hutterian Brethren. For those not living all things common, the church has also taught that believers should use wealth as a stewardship for the sake of the poor - God is still owner of all things and humans are simply managers, trustees, stewards. At times though, and particularly after the Reformation, a wedge was driven between the spiritual and the material, between the church's social teachings and economics. By abandoning its prophetic function in calling all of life to be under the Lordship of Christ, both Catholic and Protestant churches betrayed the poor and vulnerable to the forces of greed permitted by the development of markets, competition and the Industrial Revolution that came with the rise of capitalism and then European imperialism.

The social gospel movement in the late nineteenth and early twentieth century, the Catholic Church's social teachings for the last hundred years and the development of liberation theology in Latin America, beginning in the 1960s, have been attempts to recapture the prophetic spirit of solidarity with the poor. Christian Aid, Tear Fund and Cafod are among many charities attempting to redress poverty in the Third World.

Ideas for Exploration

1. Would the sun have been privatised if it had been reachable?
2. 'You shall not steal.' (Exodus 20:15 RSV). Is a rich person by definition stealing? Does a poor person steal if he or she shoplifts a loaf of bread for their children?
3. If God is creator and owner of all can a Christian believe in private property?
4. Can you be rich and a Christian?

A HINDU VIEW OF COMMITMENT TO A CULTURE OF SOLIDARITY AND A JUST ECONOMIC ORDER

Rama whose arms reached to his knees, the powerful elder brother of Lakshmana, ruled the earth in glory and performed many sacrifices with his sons, brothers, and kinsfolk. No widow was ever found in distress nor was there any danger from snakes or disease during his reign; there were no malefactors in his kingdom nor did any suffer harm; no aged person ever attended the funeral of a younger relative; happiness was universal; each attended to his duty and they had only to look to Rama to give up enmity. Men lived for a thousand years, each having a thousand sons who were free from infirmity and anxiety; trees bore fruit and flowers perpetually; Parjanya sent down rain when it was needed and Maruta blew auspiciously; all works undertaken bore happy results and all engaged in their respective duties and eschewed evil. All were endowed with good qualities; all were devoted to pious observances, and Rama ruled over the kingdom for ten thousand years.

Ramayana, Yuddha Kanda 130

Concepts of Hindu interlinkedness provide an element of basic solidarity from which Hindus cannot free themselves in principle at any one time. In the same breath, however, one has to say that this conceptual interlinkedness and ultimate equality as 'created beings' is contrasted by real disparities in wealth, power and status, of which every Hindu is also aware

As always, the ideal is to find a harmonising balance. This leads us to Hindu concepts of charity, the meritorious act of giving (*dana*), and a general understanding that any property that one owns is not in fact absolutely one's own anyway, because people cannot take their wealth with them when they die. Thus, Hindus have evolved complex ideas about individual ownership of property (for males and females) as well as joint family property. As in other non-western cultures, there is a general awareness that the living hold their property in trust for the next generation. This creates a certain sense of detachment and ultimately the ideal that one should not hunger for property, which comes out in the ideal of non-possession (*aparigraha*).

So, resourceful individuals will share a bit of their wealth with others (and will feel good about it) but inequalities persist. Modern India is, however, not unusual in having very rich and desperately poor people living side by side. Solidarity demands that the rich should share some of their wealth and should be concerned about their less fortunate neighbours. Human selfishness often interferes with this ideal, but charitable giving seems well-recognised as an element of Hindu culture.

At a more official level, concepts of a just economy have meant that modern India became a socialist republic in which individual and corporate self-control are given much emphasis, for example in a new consumer protection law which favours the small consumer over big business and emphasises public interest rather than private profit. Honest dealing in business is promoted by what is called Gandhian business ethics, after Mahatma Gandhi.

As a consequence, in modern Indian commercial and public law, the Hindu ideal of solidarity and a just economy have been put in secular language but still contain the same basic message : Self-control is necessary to achieve a functioning global order. In the field of environmental protection, too, such concepts have been powerful: an individual cannot just be allowed to pollute the environment and leave others to suffer. Environmental consciousness is clearly an ancient Hindu value which is being revived today and fits well into a global ethical framework of solidarity.

A prominent Hindu conceptualisation of this comes out as an image of the big fish devouring the small fish. If the big fish in their greed devour all the small ones, they are going to perish themselves. We can apply this to our current debates about overfishing, and other issues of great importance. The ancient Hindu law had no better response than to say that the ruler should watch over the scenario and keep the big fish in check. We are back to the issue of who controls abuses of beautiful principles! The global ethics system seems to be more dependent on everyone's self-restraint than the text admits.

The Castes

The origin of caste is lost in obscurity. Its purpose, however, seems to have been the same as that of Plato's division of the State into three classes, castes, or professions, *viz.*, philosopher-rulers, warriors and masses. The underlying principle is division of labour. Originally the castes were professional and subsequently became hereditary. The system was evolved to keep the social fabric in a harmonious condition; but in later ages it became a divisive force.

The *Rig-veda* describes the four classes as having come out of the different limbs of the body of the Creator, and thus shows the organic relation between one class and another. They are not intended to be warring communities but complementary classes. If the hands quarrel with the stomach or the head, it is not the stomach or head alone that suffers but the entire body including the hands. The head cannot claim superiority over the feet simply because it trails in the air while the latter tread the dust; the feet are as essential to the body as the head. It is the principle of integration and co-ordination that weighed with the builders of caste. 'It is a law of spiritual economics', said Mahatma Gandhi, 'It has nothing to do with superiority or inferiority'

T.M.P. Mahadevan, *Outlines of Hinduism*, p 68–70

Question

How do we ensure that everyone shows the necessary self-restraint to create a just economic order?

A JEWISH VIEW OF COMMITMENT TO A CULTURE OF SOLIDARITY AND A JUST ECONOMIC ORDER

At the festival of Sukkot Jews remember the forty years spent in the wilderness and also give thanks for the harvest. © Mark Simmons

Judaism believes that society exists on the basis that all contribute to it and all are considered entitled to protection from it. If all are considered as made in God's image then you cannot ill treat another person made just as much in God's image as yourself.

The Bible and later Jewish literature emphasise the importance of maintaining real justice in the courts, without bias to either poor or rich, as one of the keystones of a just society. Just relations between employer and employee, just behaviour to vulnerable members of society like the blind and deaf and economic provision for the poor are also key parts of creating a society which shows solidarity with all its members.

> 'When you reap the harvest of your land, you shall not reap your field to its very border, neither shall you gather the gleanings after your harvest. And you shall not strip your vineyard bare, neither shall you gather the fallen grapes of your vineyard; you shall leave them for the poor and for the sojourner; I am the Eternal your God. You shall not steal; you shall not deal deceitfully or falsely with one another . . . You shall not defraud your neighbour; you shall not steal; and you shall not keep for yourself the wages of a labourer until morning. You shall not revile the deaf or put a stumbling block before the blind; you shall fear your God; I am the Eternal. You shall not render an unjust judgement; you shall not be partial to the poor or defer to the great; with justice you shall judge your neighbour . . . You shall not falsify measures of length, weight or capacity. You shall have an honest balance, honest weights, an honest ephah, and an honest hin. (Leviticus 19:9–15, 35)

The creation of a just economic order is also a vital part of creating a just society. The book of Leviticus provides for a much more radical redistribution of property than any practised in our society

70

Then you shall have the trumpet sounded loud; on the tenth day of the seventh month - on the day of atonement - you shall have the trumpet sounded throughout all your land. And you shall hallow the fiftieth year and you shall proclaim liberty throughout the land to all its inhabitants. It shall be a jubilee for you: you shall return, every one of you, to your property and every one of you to your family. That fiftieth year shall be a jubilee for you: you shall not sow, or reap the aftergrowth, or harvest the unpruned vines. In this year of jubilee you shall return, every one of you to your property. When you make a sale to your neighbour or buy from your neighbour, you shall not cheat one another. When you buy from your neighbour, you shall pay only for the number of years since the jubilee; the seller shall charge you only for the remaining crop years. If the years are more, you shall increase the price, and if the years are fewer, you shall diminish the price; for it is a certain number of harvests that are being sold to you. (Leviticus 25:9-16)

No land sale could be permanent: land was sold for the value of the harvests between then and the jubilee and then it returned to the original owner.

There is a great deal of writing in later Jewish literature on business ethics and responsibilities between an employer and his workers. A sixth century Jewish legal text says:

The first question a man is asked in the world to come: Were you honest in your business dealings? (Talmud Shabbat 31a)

Another legal text says

Someone who destroys another person's livelihood by unfair competition is like an adulterer (Talmud Sanhedrin 81a)

To understand the significance of this quote, one must remember that adultery is one of the most serious sins a Jew can commit.

Some Examples of Jewish Teaching

A worker must not work at night at his own work and then hire himself out during the day; nor plough with his cow in the evenings and hire her out in the mornings; nor should he go hungry and afflict himself in order to feed his children - for by so doing he steals labour from his employer.

. . . He who withholds a worker's wages is as though he deprived him of his life . . . If a person hires workers and asks them to work in the early morning or late evening at a place where it is not the local custom to work early or late at night, he cannot force them to do so. In a place where it is customary to provide food for workers he must do so. In a place where the employer feeds his workers two courses, an employer may not feed his workers only one course . . . If someone hires employees and then discovers that he has not enough work for them, how should they be paid? Not at the skilled workers' rate, but as one who has had his time occupied. (Talmud Baba Metziah)

Just as the employer is told not to deprive the poor worker of his wages or to withhold them from him when they are due, so the worker is enjoined not to deprive the employer of the benefit of his work by idling away his time, a little here and a little there, thus wasting the whole day deceitfully . . . indeed the worker must be very punctual in the matter of time. (Maimonides' Mishneh Torah [12th century code of Jewish law] Laws Concerning Hiring).

Buyers and sellers must also behave in an ethical way to each other if the economic affairs of society are to be conducted in a way that increases the sense of justice within society.

One must be careful not to cheat one's neighbour, whether he is a seller or a buyer. If one has something to sell, he is forbidden to make it look better than it really is, in order to deceive the customer . . . A customer entering a shop should not ask the price of goods if he is sure that he will not buy anything, because he raises the shopkeeper's hopes.
(Shulchan Aruch, 16th century code of Jewish law).

Questions:

1. Why is having a reliable system of justice and courts which give fair verdicts to all one of the key factors in creating a society in which there is solidarity for all its members?

2. Why is it important for both employer and employee to have responsibilities towards each other?

3. What do you think are important issues for employers and employees in our society?

4. What other important ethical questions should buyers and sellers be careful about?

5. What could be a way of implementing the Jubilee of Leviticus in our society?

6. Leviticus speaks of not cursing the deaf or putting a stumbling block before the blind. What else do we have to do to give those who are physically disabled a just place in society?

A MUSLIM VIEW OF COMMITMENT TO A CULTURE OF SOLIDARITY AND A JUST ECONOMIC ORDER

Allah commands justice, the doing of good and liberality to kith and kin, and he forbids all shameful deeds, and injustice and rebellion, he instructs you, that ye may receive admonition.

Qur'an 16:90

O you who have attained to faith: be ever steadfast in your devotion to God, bearing witness to the truth in all equity; and never let hatred of anyone lead you into the sin of deviating from justice. Be just: this is closest to being God-conscious. And remain conscious of God; verily, God is aware of all that you do.

Qur'an 5:8

Zakat

The fourth pillar of Islam is *zakat*, or spiritual tithing and alms giving. At the end of the year, all Muslims must donate at least two and a half per cent of their income (after basic expenses) to needy Muslims. This provision is designed to help even out inequalities in wealth and to prevent personal greed. Its literal meaning is 'purity', for it purifies the distribution of money; helping to keep it in healthy circulation.

Quoted from Mary Pat Fisher and Robert Luyster, *Living Religions*, p. 294

How do we achieve a just economy and solidarity with others? Solidarity which I suppose means recognising each others' common links as human beings is the same as respecting each other as the creation of God. As Muslims we are exhorted to be just even if it is against our own interests or those of our family and friends. 'Be just: this is the closest to being God-conscious. I may not buy cheaply something of value if the seller is ignorant of the worth of the goods. I must inform him of the fair price and pay it.' We are instructed in the Holy Qur'an not to use sophisticated legal means to deprive others. 'And devour not one another's possessions wrongly, neither employ legal artifices with a view to devouring sinfully, and knowingly, anything that by right belongs to another.'

A just and fair economy should nowadays be very much a global matter. In Islam usury is forbidden. This is a complicated area and Muslim scholars are applying themselves to formulating a religiously satisfactory approach to modern business practices and investment. They are convinced that the Third World debt with its huge interest rate is usurious and therefore sinful as it is harming the world. In a just economy everyone should receive adequate food, housing, health care, education and anything else good that is normal in the society in which they live. The Qur'an stresses that those of us who are given more wealth, ability and education must use them for the benefit of those in need. Almsgiving is one of the five pillars of Islam. What we own is only as vice-regents under God and should be shared. We know that Muhammad lived a simple life even when he was Head of State and refused to live at a higher standard than the poorest in the community.

How can we bring about a just economy? Apart from the normal political process, we need to be aware that self-interest sometimes acts against our eventual benefit. As Muslims we are always advised to start with what is nearest to us and therefore more capable of change.

Question

Do you think it is wrong to lend money for interest?

Do you think the rich nations should cancel 'Third World debt'?

A RASTAFARIAN VIEW OF COMMITMENT TO A CULTURE OF SOLIDARITY AND A JUST ECONOMIC ORDER

Most Rastafarians will have no difficulty identifying with the call for solidarity in the Global Ethic. This principle is fundamental to Rastafarian doctrine, which dictates one-ness with the Creator, Jah Rastafari; one-ness with the Creation and one-ness with self. In essence this means' living in harmony and equilibrium, ensuring that the Inity (unity) of the whole is preserved. This concept of living is rooted in the Kamitic (ancient Egyptian) 'Six Acts of Creation', the second of which is the means of enforcing order. The fundamental principle of order is that no thing can encroach on another (respect for the rights of the other). However overlying this principle is the fundamental that, although all things are protected, the main interest is the preservation of the whole. In essence, the basis of order is one-ness of origin. In Rasta doctrine this represents the coming together of the whole.

In the Kamitic tradition, beyond external differences between things there is paramount emphasis on their inter-dependence. For many Rastas, this one-ness in the midst of difference is the state of 'Inity' ('Equilibrium and Order'), which is the foundation of good, whilst disunity or the state of 'Men' is the basis of evil. The concept of 'I' involves equilibrium being established between the whole and the individual; man and woman; elder and youth and the objective and the subjective. This results in solidarity. This concept is to be found in the Swahili word 'Imoja' (one).

In the Rastafarian world view, order can only be restored by solidarity between Rastas, the broader African world and oppressed peoples everywhere. The framing and enforcement of laws and universal declarations cannot of themselves bring about this state of order and equilibrium. It can only be brought about by acquiring knowledge of 'Self', which cannot be attained by study and research alone, but more importantly by inward reflection and experience. Self knowledge encompasses all knowledge. Hence many Rastas do not consider their doctrine a religion based on belief in the Western sense, but one of knowledge.

In the context of a just economic order, this means solidarity/equilibrium from the pooling of resources in a harmonious and co-operative manner. In the Bahamas this tradition is found in the 'Asue', a customary co-operative banking system, which is utilised by not only Rastas, but also by the broader community. In Swahili the words 'Ujaama' (collective work and effort) and 'Ujima' (co-operative economics), closely convey the essence of this Rastafarian ideal of wealth. This philosophy is reflected in Hindu and traditional African societies, namely the concept of property being held in trust, passed on from ancestor to successive generations. This is demonstrated in the Bahamian customary law institution of 'Generation Property'. which operates outside and unrecognised by the official legal system. This concept of property is in contradistinction to Western concepts, which reduce property and wealth to individual dimensions. Within this framework, most if not all Rastafarians can identify with the irrevocable directive that one should deal honestly, fairly, and not steal.

The Rastafarian ethos is demonstrated by the saying 'To eat from your own vineyard is sweet to the stomach. To steal from your brethren is bitter to the belly'. To steal or be dishonest in one's dealings are acts of disunity, upsetting the equilibrium and inevitably it will lead to spiritual and physical death.

However concepts of 'honesty' and 'theft' are not as clear cut as assumed in the Global Ethic and must be placed in context. In the Book of Genesis (27:1-39) Jacob obtained blessings from the Patriarch Isaac, by covering his body with a hairy hide, thereby deceiving Isaac into giving him the blessing that by right belonged to Esau. Hence Isaac, whose eyesight had failed him, considered that the blessing was obtained by fraud. It was not withdrawn however and Jacob became Israel. Similarly, in the Kebra Negast we see that the Ark of the Covenant was stolen by Levites, who had been sent by Solomon to Ethiopia to accompany his son Menelik I. Jah not only condoned this act, but prevented Solomon from ever recovering the Ark. This ethos is reflected in the West Indian stories of Anansi the spider man. He constantly gained advantage on the basis of his quick wit. In one such story he steals a pot of stew from Tiger (a risky endeavour) to feed his starving family.

All of these stories illustrate Rasta principles of 'equilibrium and order'. In the case of Jacob, Esau had earlier sold his birthright for a meal of lentils and bread, thereby demonstrating the low esteem in which he held it. In the case of King Solomon, he had earlier been visited by Queen Sheba who sought instruction about the God of Israel. Rather than giving her religious instruction, he tricked her into having sexual relations with him. In the case of Anansi, Tiger was a destructive tyrant and no doubt his greed contributed to the starving state of Anansi's family.

For many Rastas, the enslavement of the African people and the colonial exploitation of resources by Western nations represents dishonest behaviour and theft. The West are today reaping the benefits of these acts of dishonesty and theft. For many Rastas this raises the issue of reparations for the African people (at home and abroad) and the failure of the Global Ethic to address this issue will be seen by many as proof that this document has failed to come to terms with historical realities. Until reparations are made to the African people then natural order and equilibrium will remain disrupted. Many foresee the only likely result will be the ultimate collapse of the West and its financial systems. As long as the West fails to come to terms with its role in the exploitation of the African people, many Rastas will view with suspicion Western moral rearmament and the conceptualisation of moral ethics. This leads to another concern: who is to enforce this 'Global Ethic'? This concern for me is intensified by the use of terms such as 'authentic human', 'fully human life' and 'tolerance'. The poor and the weak need to be protected. Many Rastas can readily identify with the concepts of consumer protection laws being developed in Indian jurisprudence. In contrast to Western jurisprudence, which generally reduces justice to the realm of individual as opposed to collective rights and obligations, the Indian legal system is demonstrating how law can help to restore equilibrium and order, without which there can be no global culture of solidarity and no just economic order. No justice! No peace!

Question

How do you think the Western and the Rastafarian concepts of property differ?

Do you think the West should make reparations to Africa for the slave-trade and colonialism? What form might such reparations take?

ੴ

A SIKH VIEW OF COMMITMENT TO A CULTURE OF SOLIDARITY AND A JUST ECONOMY

One who lives by earning through hard work, then gives some of it away in charity, knows the way to God.

Guru Nanak: GGS-1245

Three Principles of the Sikh Faith.

Meditation and prayer.

Earning an honest living through hard work.

Sharing it with others and service to others.

Five Key Weaknesses

Kaam (lust)

Krodh (anger)

Lobh (greed)

Moh (attachment/ possessiveness)

Ahunkar (Ego)

Lust and anger deteriorate the body as borax melts gold.

GGS-932

O God, rid us of lust, anger, greed and lies.

Guru Arjan: GGS-932

Truth is the foremost, but higher than truth is truthful living.

Japji Sahib: GGS-1

Living by those principles taught by the Gurus helps to remove egoism and fosters commitment to fellow human beings and to the world around. The weaknesses listed in column one not only affect human beings at an individual level but have major effects on creating divisions among groups on a social and ethnic basis, between classes and castes, races, nations and religions and cause suffering. A Sikh should work towards removing them. The way to overcoming them is to lead one's life according to the Guru's teachings and the principles of the faith.

A Sikh, who works hard to earn a living in accordance with the faith tradition, is not likely to exploit others. Living by the principle of selfless service and sharing can enable people to help alleviate hunger, poverty and need. It is, however, becoming increasingly difficult for many Sikhs to live up to the Sikh principles particularly in the West where they may be without work, exploited by poor wages or forced to the edges of society. Materialism, against which the Gurus consistently cautioned Sikhs and exploitation of others are issues affecting the social fabric and the spiritual well being of people. Corruption in society is making the weak weaker. Many Sikhs feel that they are finding it more and more difficult to help the weaker to become full participants in society.

The Sikhs believe that the other name for God is 'Truth'. Truthful living, if practised would make it virtually impossible to steal. Acting on this principle would encourage dealing honestly and fairly with others. Robbing others of their possession and using ones' own resources for self, is not the Sikh way. There are many stories in the lives of the Guru's in which they showed the path to true business and true work, earning one's living with honesty and hard work.

The Sikh Gurus taught that those who are more fortunate should help the needy, raise them to be equal and see the divine in them.

Sikh Rulers, particularly Maharaja Ranjit Singh of Punjab (1799-1839) have shown by example that we must utilise economic and political power for service to humanity.

There should be balance. Compassion and care for those who cannot fend for themselves. Everybody should be treated with mutual respect and dignity regardless of

It is the duty of adults to encourage young people whether at home and at school to learn to care for and make responsible use of property for the benefits of everybody. They are our stewards for the future just economic order.

A poor person's mouth is God's treasure chest.

The Lord stands for us if we are not usurpers.

He who strokes his beard before the poor, God will burn it in fire.

Guru Arjjan: GGS-199

(The above 3 quotations taken from Guru Granth Sahib show the way to God through the service of the poor. A person who shows off in front of God will not be spared by God. Exploitation of others is forbidden in the same way as pork is for Muslims and beef is for Hindus.)

status or caste. Resources should not be used for the benefit of the individual or nation but for the common good of all. That is why there is a system of langar, community kitchen, in which high and low, rich and poor, young and old, women and men can share food at an equal level in the Sikh place of worship, The Gurdwara.

STORY OF BHAI LALO AND MALIK BHAGO

Guru Nanak visited Eminabad in Gujranwala district (now in Pakistan) in 1497, and decided to stay with a carpenter named Lalo. He earned his living through honest hard work. Though a poor man who lived within his means, he was very contented and cheerful. The Guru was quite happy with the simple food he was served with devotion by Lalo.

The news got round that the high caste Guru was staying with a lowly person. Malik Bhago, the high caste corrupt treasurer of the local ruler, became very upset because the Guru was bringing a bad name to his high caste community. Messages were sent for the Guru to stay somewhere suitable, but he declined and continued to live simply, spending his time in meditation and prayer.

Once Malik Bhago arranged a big feast to celebrate a family event. He invited holy men from far and near, so that he could receive their blessings to become more rich. Guru Nanak was also invited, but he declined to attend. When Malik Bhago heard about this, he sent his officials to bring the Guru to his place forcibly. There the Guru was reprimanded by Malik Bhago for not coming to the feast. The Guru calmly picked a piece of bread from Malik Bhago's tray and another piece of bread that Lalo had made. It is said that milk poured out of Lalo's bread whereas Malik Bhago's reeked of blood when he gave them a little squeeze. The Guru explained that the earnings by hard work of a pious man are pure and earning through corrupt means, bribery and use of force will remain stained with the blood of the poor and weak. In a very unusual way, Guru Banak showed that exploiting people is wrong and we should work towards fairness and sharing.

Ideas for exploration

What lessons can be learnt from the story of Bhago and Bhai Lalo?

Why is a poor person's mouth God's treasure chest? How can Sikh principles help to create solidarity and a just economic order?

A ZOROASTRIAN VIEW OF COMMITMENT TO A CULTURE OF SOLIDARITY AND A JUST ECONOMIC ORDER

O, Wise Jamaspa of Hvogvas family, learn this point that movement and activity are better than laziness and inactivity. Therefore, worship Him with full conscience and good deeds. Worship Ahura Mazda, who discerns the wise from the unwise and is Guardian of This World.

GY 46, 17

A just society is one where people treat each other with respect and fairness, caring about and considering the needs of individuals who are less fortunate than themselves. In so far as there is compassion and consideration for everyone, and this is reflected both in the legislation and the social interaction, such a society may be described as showing solidarity for its fellow humans.

At the base of most people's daily concerns is the concern to have food, shelter and clothing. To achieve this most people engage in work which is in fact a means of exchange: in return for a service I do for you, you pay me either in food, clothing or else in money which will enable me to purchase my needs. If the person offering work is fair, decent, honest and compassionate, s/he will not try and exploit the person who may desperately need to work. However, someone who does not listen to his *conscience*, will not choose the path of **asha** (truth and righteousness), and will try and take advantage of the person in the weaker position.

To allow a community to function harmoniously, it is necessary that both the provider of work and the person undertaking the work agree on the terms and that the terms are just. An ethic based on honesty and integrity, **asha,** should ensure that both the provider and the giver of work will be satisfied about the conditions of work. However, there is always a section of society who cannot undertake work: disabled people, those with psychiatric disorders, mothers bringing up children, and those who simply have not managed to find a way of providing for themselves. In Zoroastrian teaching, we cannot simply ignore them. We have a duty towards them as fellow humans and we should not forget their needs in concerning ourselves with ours.

For this reason, Zoroastrians are expected to work hard, to make an honest living, if possible to provide work for others by offering decent conditions, and certainly to make charitable donations to benefit others. Zoroastrians are also taught to be thrifty and not to waste resources. Undoubtedly this is partially a result of years of suffering and hardship but the principle allows savings to be made which can be put to use to benefit others. In a similar way, wealthy Zoroastrians are not expected to be ostentatious but to quietly go about their business maintaining the teaching of *moderation* in all things.

These teachings have been institutionalised by creating

The path, O Ahura, which Thou hast shown me is the path of Vohuman, the path based on the teachings of Saoshyants, the saviours. The teaching recommends that work performed with the view of performing one's duty honestly shall bring forth happiness. The teaching leads mankind to real knowledge and wisdom.

Those persons would enjoy that precious reward which has been promised, O Mazda, who perform actions through knowledge and pure thought; who strive for the progress and development of the world; fulfil God's desire and try for the progress of God's Will through truth and righteousness.

GY 34, 13–14

6 periods a year known as *gahambar* when charitable memorial feasts lasting 5 days each ensure that food is distributed to everyone in the community, thus creating a bond of solidarity. Additionally, of course, this at least provides a guaranteed amount of food on a regular basis, which is distributed in significantly larger quantities to those who are known to be in need. The foods are usually storeable, (e.g. dried fruit, nuts, sweets and bread which can be stored as crispbread). On a more modest scale any person who has experienced a wish coming true will often give a communal feast, ranging from a distribution of spiced and nutty fried bread, to a substantial meat and vegetable stew.

Where Zoroastrians have risen to prominence and made fortunes as they did in India in the 19th and 20th century, and in Iran in the late twentieth century, the charitable donations take the form of orphanages, schools, hospitals, hostels, housing units etc. which provide a service not only to Zoroastrians but to the wider community. They also create employment with decent conditions of work and pay, which is considered meritorious. Philanthropic Zoroastrians are certainly well known amongst people of the sub-continent of India.

A just and caring society is not only one where work takes place, but is also one where life is enjoyed. Pleasure is a fundamental part of Zoroastrian philosophy. The creation of the Wise Lord, **Ahura Mazda**, is to be appreciated and enjoyed. Thus the creation of festivals and feasts as occasions for enjoying the company of each other, and giving thanks to the Creator for the bounties on earth punctuate the life of a Zoroastrian on a regular basis. During festivals which celebrate the discovery of fire, the presence of rain and water, the arrival of Spring and the New Year life cycle, the bringing in of the harvest, laughter, singing and music, dancing and merriment, with the aid of wine is the order of the day. In this way the hardship of daily life is lightened with an occasion to look forward to.

To consider

Try to find out how much the people who grow tea and coffee earn? Do people in the West pay a fair price or are they exploiting the poor in other parts of the world?

What occasions do you celebrate?

Do the celebrations involve the disadvantaged?

79

The Third Directive is:

Commitment to a culture of tolerance and a life of truthfulness

A BAHA'I VIEW OF COMMITMENT TO A CULTURE OF TOLERANCE AND A LIFE OF TRUTHFULNESS

A fundamental principle announced by the Prophet Baha'u'llah is that of the unity of humankind. Since all people share in the same humanity, there should be no room for prejudice between people - in fact, his message to the world is that all should deal with everyone in the spirit of unity, promoting friendship, honour and conciliation.

- Be compassionate and kind to all the human race.
- Deal with strangers the same as with friends.
- Cherish others just as you would your own.
- Beware lest you harm any soul or make any heart to sorrow
- Beware lest any of you seek vengeance.
- Beware lest you offend the feelings of another.
- See no-one as your enemy; wish no-one ill.
- Pray for all; ask that all be blessed, and all forgiven.

The Baha'i Shrine of the Bab or 'the Gate' (1819-1850), at Haifa, Israel.

Consort with the followers of all religions in a spirit of friendliness and fellowship.

Baha'u'llah *Tablets of Baha'u'llah* 35

In the eyes of the Creator all His children are equal; His goodness is poured forth on all. He does not favour this nation nor that nation, all alike are His creatures. This being so, why should we make divisions, separating one race from another? Why should we create barriers of superstition and tradition bringing discord and hatred among the people?

'Abdu'l-Baha, *Paris Talks* 138

The light of a good character surpasseth the light of the sun.

Baha'u'llah, *Tablets of Baha'u'llah* 36

The ills of the world relate to another fundamental principle announced by Baha'u' llah - that of the oneness of religion.

The Baha'i view is that there is one God, the creator of all, and the focus of the world's religions. It follows, then, that if all worship the one God, and all religions have the same basic aim to promote knowledge of the Divine, there should be concord and unity between peoples and faiths.

The Prophet also said that the fundamental purpose of religion is to safeguard the interests and promote the unity of the human race, and to foster the spirit of love and fellowship among people. When there is lack of religious unity the result is enmity and alienation rather than agreement and fellowship.

? What practical steps can you, or your group, take to improve religious unity?

'O thou kind Lord! Unite all. Let the religions agree and make the nations one, so that they may see each other as one family and the whole earth as one home. May they all live together in perfect harmony.'

(From a prayer of 'Abdu'l-Baha, *Baha'i Prayers* 103)

There can be no doubt whatever that the peoples of the world, of whatever race or religion, derive their inspiration from one heavenly Source, and are the subjects of one God. The difference between the ordinances under which they abide should be attributed to the varying requirements and exigencies of the age in which they were revealed. All of them, except a few which are the outcome of human perversity, were ordained of God, and are a reflection of His Will and Purpose.

Baha'u'llah, *Gleanings from the Writings of Baha'ullah* 217

Sincerity is the foundation-stone of faith. That is, a religious individual must disregard his personal desires and seek in whatever way he can wholeheartedly to serve the public interest; and it is impossible for a human being to turn aside from his own selfish advantages and sacrifice his own good for the good of the community except through true religious faith.

'Abdu'l-Baha, *Secret of Divine Civilization* 96

What profit is there in agreeing that universal friendship is good, and talking of the solidarity of the human race as a grand ideal? Unless these thoughts are translated into the world of action, they are useless.

'Abdu'l-Baha *Paris Talks* 16

The best beloved of all things in My sight is Justice.

Baha'u'llah, *Hidden Words* 2

The fruits of the tree of man have ever been and are goodly deeds and a praiseworthy character.

Baha'u'llah, *Epistle to the Son of the Wolf* 26

A life of truthfulness and honesty in this physical world is an essential requirement if one wishes to perfect one's character in preparation for the spiritual world to come.

The following words of Baha'u'llah describe such a spiritually-based life in this beautiful meditation.

Be generous in prosperity, and thankful in adversity.

Be worthy of the trust of thy neighbour, and look upon him with a bright and friendly face.

Be a treasure to the poor, an admonisher to the rich, an answerer of the cry of the needy, a preserver of the sanctity of thy pledge.

Be fair in thy judgement, and guarded in thy speech.

Be unjust to no man, and show all meekness to all men.

Be as a lamp unto them that walk in darkness, a joy to the sorrowful, a sea for the thirsty, a haven for the distressed, an upholder and defender of the victim of oppression.

Let integrity and uprightness distinguish all thine acts.

Be a home for the stranger, a balm to the suffering, a tower of strength for the fugitive.

Be eyes to the blind, and a guiding light unto the feet of the erring.

Be an ornament to the countenance of truth, a crown to the brow of fidelity, a pillar of the temple of righteousness, a breath of life to the body of mankind, an ensign of the hosts of justice, a luminary above the horizon of virtue, a dew to the soil of the human heart, an ark on the ocean of knowledge, a sun in the heaven of bounty, a gem on the diadem of wisdom, a shining light in the firmament of thy generation, a fruit upon the tree of humility.

(*Gleanings from the Writings of Baha'u'llah* 285)

A BRAHMA KUMARIS VIEW OF COMMITMENT TO A CULTURE OF TOLERANCE AND A LIFE OF TRUTHFULNESS

Think of an aspect of truth that is meaningful for you. How may you increase its application in your life?

The first kind of honesty is honesty with myself. If I am honest with myself, there need be no situation in which I am not honest with others. (Companion of God)

Honesty is a clear conscience 'before myself and before my fellow human beings'. Honesty is the awareness of what is right and appropriate in one's role, one's behaviour and one's relationships. With honesty there is no hypocrisy or artificiality, which create confusion and mistrust in the minds of others. Honesty makes for a life of integrity because the inner and outer selves are a mirror image. (Living Values)

Honesty is to speak that which is thought and to do that which is spoken. There are no contradictions or discrepancies in thoughts, words, or actions. Such integration provides clarity and example to others. To have one form internally and another form externally creates barriers and can cause damage, since one would neither be able to come close to anyone else, nor would others want to be close. Some think, 'I am honest, but no-one understands me.' That is not honest. Honesty is as distinct as a flawless diamond which can never remain hidden. The worth is visible in one's actions. (Living Values)

Truthfulness

For students of the Brahma Kumaris World Spiritual University, truthfulness is a fundamental principle of life: truthfulness with the self, others and God. A life of truthfulness is a life that is worthwhile and filled with beauty, because included in truthfulness is honesty and selflessness. Truthfulness together with love creates tolerance and harmony. In a potential situation of conflict, truthfulness can change the atmosphere and ultimately result in understanding, acceptance and love. However, to be truthful takes courage and strength. A foundation of truth is required to provide us with the method or the 'how to' of truthfulness and tolerance.

Important truths leading to a life of truthfulness and tolerance include:

- I am a soul, a child of God, part of the family of humanity;
- The soul, in its original state, is filled with love, peace, wisdom, happiness and strength;
- This original state is true for each and every human being; thus there is inherent good in everyone;
- Every soul has an eternal relationship with God and can avail themselves of God's love, mercy and forgiveness.

When these fundamental truths are practised in life (in thoughts, feelings, words and actions) then inequality, hatred, disrespect and intolerance are counteracted. These truths enable one to develop an attitude of humility and self respect, and the ability to learn from life's challenges.

If the awareness of these truths is less, then arrogance, based on external identities (such as role or position in the family or at work, etc.) takes over our awareness. This leads to a lack of truthfulness within the self as we try to uphold these identities, sometimes at the cost of hurting others and ourselves. We may be tempted to use unethical behaviour, or try to control or manipulate people or situations in an attempt to cover up our mistakes or to hold on to our position and power. It becomes difficult to learn from constructive criticism or to accept genuine offers of help. Instead we tend to blame others for our own shortcomings. To face the truth is sometimes painful and requires strength.

An honest person is one who aspires to follow the highest codes of conduct, who is loyal to the benevolent and universal principles of life, and whose decisions are based clearly on what is right and wrong. (Living Values)

To be trusted and to trust provide the foundation and cohesion necessary for untarnished relationships. It is also necessary to share with honesty the feelings and motives of one another. Where there is honesty and cleanliness, there is also closeness. Without these principles, neither individuals nor societies can be functional. (Living Values)

Honesty is never to misuse that which is given in trust. (Living Values)

Becoming Truthful

How can we acquire the strength to be truthful? To recognise, accept and live by truth, we need clarity and the ability to discern. We need to put aside things that may interfere with our ability to perceive the truth.

Forgetting the Past

One of the first things we need to do is to free ourselves from the negative influence of the past. Thinking about the past over and over again, brings up feelings of unhappiness and it is difficult for the mind to focus on the present or future. Bringing to mind the important truths mentioned above, helps us to use the mind in a positive and productive way, so that negative thoughts of the past abate. Then we can put a full stop to those troubling thoughts and move ahead with clarity.

Being God's Companion

Having gained some clarity, we now need to consider a source of strength that we can draw from to be able to live in truth. The highest source of strength and of all that is good, is God. Why shouldn't we choose the best for ourselves and become God's companion? When God is with us and we are with God, the impossible becomes possible.

It is said that *'the one who has truth constantly dances in happiness'*. In the company of the truth life is filled with happiness and we enjoy God's protection and guidance. There is reality in our awareness and behaviour, as we are able to take all the spiritual treasures that we need from God. There is true self-respect and we celebrate life with enthusiasm.

In the company of the Truth, our every thought, word and action is filled with truth and spiritual strength. As powerful seeds bear good fruit, so our thoughts, words and actions filled with truth, will take practical form, giving happiness and strength to others. Integrity and divinity are visible in our life as an inspiration to others. This is true success in life.

A BUDDHIST VIEW OF COMMITMENT TO A CULTURE OF TOLERANCE AND A LIFE OF TRUTHFULNESS.

The Buddha advised..

'.. do not be led by reports, or by tradition, or hearsay. Do not be led by the authority of religious texts, nor by mere logic or inference, nor by considering appearances, nor by the delight in speculative opinions, nor by seeming possibilities, nor by the idea 'this is our teacher'. But when you know for yourselves that certain things are unwhole-some and wrong and bad, then give them up. And when you know for yourselves certain things are wholesome and good, then accept them and follow them'.
Vimamsaka sutta

King Priyadarshi honours men of all faith, members of religious orders and laymen alike, with gifts and various marks of esteem. Yet he does not value either gifts or honours as much as growth in the qualities essential to religion in men of all faiths.

This growth may take many forms, but its root is in guarding one's speech to avoid extolling one's own faith and disparaging the faith of others improperly or, when the occasion is appropriate, immoderately.

The faiths of others all deserve to be honoured for one reason or another. By honouring them, one exalts one's own faith and at the same time performs a service to the faith of others. By acting otherwise, one injures one's own faith and also does disservice to that of others. For if a man extols his own faith and disparages another because of devotion to his own and because he wants to glorify it, he seriously injures his own faith.

How do we know where to look for the truth ?

The teachings of the Buddha (the 'awakened one') were not based on any external authority, such as a divine revelation, but came from his own experience of complete liberation from delusion and suffering, which he invited others to find for themselves. Buddhism is a path, a method, not a set of answers.

The Buddha 'set in motion the wheel of the Teaching' and it has been growing for 2,500 years, finding more and more 'skilful means'. There are said to be 84,000 doors to the Truth. This has produced a great many schools and traditions, all disputing as to whose method is best, but no-one having the claim to a monopoly, or a 'last word'.

Since Buddhism is the path to wisdom and compassion, anything which helps someone along the way should be acceptable, whether it is classed as Buddhist or non-Buddhist. In fact, Buddhism has frequently merged with other religions, or existed alongside them. The first Precept forbids violence, so using force against people with other views would already mean you had left the Buddhist path.

Tolerance has been intrinsic to Buddhism and has meant that it has allowed itself to be destroyed in many countries rather than resist. Today, Tibetans are faced with a terrible choice, to see their way of life and religion destroyed by the Chinese occupation of their country, or go against their Precepts by fighting with weapons. Non-violence is not an easy option.

Words are not the same as the Truth. The Buddha is said to have doubted whether his supreme insight could be conveyed in any words (although he spent his life trying). The Zen school calls its teaching 'a finger pointing at the moon' (don't look at the finger, look at the moon !).

The basic practice of all Buddhists is silent meditation. The Goal is Nirvana, a state beyond words, which the Buddha seems to have expressed by just smiling (and being).

Yet, words are important. One of the Precepts is not to tell lies; more positively we talk about Right Speech. Speech is to be used to convey positive, helpful messages that undo conflict and delusion. Lying is a kind of violence towards others and is often covering up our fear

Therefore concord alone is comendable, for through concord men may learn and respect the conception of Dharma accepted by others.

King Priyadarshi desires men of all faiths to know each other's doctrines and to acquire sound doctrines.

N. A. Nikam and Richard McKeon, Eds. *The Edicts of Asoka*, University of Chicago Press 1959, pp. 51–2.

or shame. Acting rightly, there is no need to be untruthful.

If we look beyond the facts, giving the whole truth may be unskilful or unkind, in the circumstances. We are told that the Buddha used to keep 'noble silence', when people would not be helped by an answer.

Tibetan monks debate vigorously at Sera Monastery, near Lhasa.

Questions

Do we always have to say the whole truth?

One story has the Buddha encounter a frightened deer, and then the hunters pursuing it. They asked which way it had gone. What is the right answer in this situation? The Buddha maintained that all his teachings were only to liberate living beings from suffering. So his pointing in the 'wrong' direction was actually the right answer!

How can we know what is true?

According to Buddhism, acting from delusion is always followed by suffering, 'as the cart follows the ox'. If it hurts, you have misunderstood something. But Wisdom gives rise to peace, joy and compassion for the suffering of others; you are smiling inside....

A CHRISTIAN VIEW OF COMMITMENT TO A CULTURE OF TOLERANCE AND A LIFE OF TRUTHFULNESS

You shall not bear false witness against your neighbour

Exodus 20:16

For truth without love kills, while love without truth lies.

Eberhard Arnold

And the Word became flesh and dwelt among us, full of grace and truth.

John 1:14

The first casualty in war is truth. Hear what a government says during a war. Then find what the truth really was after the war. During times of oppression, be it Stalinist Russia, Nazi Germany or dictatorships in the Third World, the truth is ruthlessly suppressed by police, military violence and by the myths of propaganda. Even in modern democracies there are cover-ups, misinformation, and in Britain, the Official Secrets Act, forbidding the telling of truth because of national security.

Myths are powerful stories. There is the myth of redemptive violence. There is the myth that violence is required to maintain social order. There is the myth that some are entitled to wealth and power and others rightly condemned to poverty. There is the myth that certain groups or individuals should be scapegoated and punished to maintain social tranquillity. These myths cover up injustice and the exploitation of the poor by the rich and powerful. In the life of Jesus we see a confrontation between these myths and truth; the exposure of systems of power and their injustice and violence. One of the great themes of John's gospel is truth and it begins with these words: 'And the Word became flesh and dwelt among us, full of grace and truth.' (John 1:14) Satan is called the 'father of lies'. 'He was a murderer from the beginning, and has nothing to do with the truth.' (John 8:44) The confrontation between light and darkness, truth and lie comes to a head when Jesus is on trial before Pilate:

> Pilate said to him 'So you are a king?' Jesus answered, 'You say that I am a king. For this I was born, and for this I have come into the world, to bear witness to the truth. Everyone who is of the truth hears my voice.' Pilate said to him 'What is truth?' (John 18:37-38)

In the crucifixion of an innocent, non-violent man, the lies that support violent, unjust systems of power and privilege are fully exposed and every claim to their legitimacy shattered. Roman imperialism and the reign of God could not be more starkly contrasted. The might of Rome is exposed by the power of unarmed suffering. W. Wink in his own translation of Paul's letter to the Colossians puts it thus:

88

If you continue in my word, you are truly my disciples, and you will know the truth and the truth will make you free.

John 8.31-32

I am the way the truth and the life. No one comes to the Father, but by me.

John 14:6

When the Spirit comes, he will guide you into all truth.

John 16:13

'Unmasking the Principalities and Powers, God publicly shames them exposing them in Christ's triumphal procession by means of the cross.' (Colossians 2:15,)[1]

The cross is being unarmed, vulnerable, witnessing. The early Christians also took up their cross to follow Jesus, risking, and in many cases enduring, martyrdom and persecution.

This contrasts vividly with later Christian history – notably the Inquisition for the correction and punishment of heretics. This shameful Christian institution belongs to the dark side of Christian history. How did it come about?

The Inquisition

The Inquisition was a medieval church court, empowered by church and state, to seek out, torture and in particular cases hand over 'heretics' for execution by the state – generally by burning at the stake. It claimed legitimacy from St. Augustine (354–430 CE) who interpreted the parable of the great messianic banquet as commanding compulsion in membership of the Christian church (Luke 14:23). Augustine was writing after Constantine the Great had at the beginning of the fourth century begun the process of making Christianity the state religion. This could be argued as a complete betrayal of Jesus' crucifixion and its exposure of systems of domination. Nevertheless, with a new emphasis on orthodoxy of belief, Augustine's teaching set the stage for the persecution of heretics, be they sects like the Albigenses and Waldenses in the twelfth century or Jews and Muslims in the fifteenth century or Protestants in the sixteenth century onwards. Although Protestants did not have an equivalent institution they also suppressed sects like the more radical Anabaptists as well as Catholics. The Spanish Inquisition, which was particularly cruel, efficient and ruthless because of its strong ties with the crown, was not ended until 1834.

The Inquisition is a major embarrassment for modern Christians. An even greater problem and shame for Christians is their historical preparation for, and The participation of some Cristians in the Nazi Holocaust of the Jews. The persecution of Jews by Christians began after Constantine. Their crime – 'deicide' – the murder of God. In the middle ages Jews, forced to be money lenders, were at the same time accused of being parasites and exploiting Christians (eg Peter the Hermit). At the same time accusations of ritual murder of Christian children – the 'Blood Libel myth' – began to appear, firstly with the

89

story of the supposed victim William of Norwich in 1144. Martin Luther, the great Protestant reformer, wrote virulently against Jews. The lies of anti-Semitism and the accompanying stereotypes created by Christians, were used in secularised form by Hitler and the Nazis to justify the holocaust in which over 6 million Jews were killed between 1938-1945.

Christians in the inquisition and the Holocaust have repeatedly broken the ninth commandment 'You shall not bear false witness against your neighbour.' Christian history should also make repentant Christians deeply suspicious of being in bed with state power. However, there are Christian witnesses who point in a more faithful direction. Consider, for example, Thomas Helwyns (c1570–1616), one of the persecuted founders of the Baptists. He argued for freedom of conscience thus:

> Men's religion to God is betwixt God and themselves; the king shall not answer for it, neither may the king be judge between God and Man. Let them be heretics, Turks, Jews or whatsoever, it appertains not to the earthy powers to punish them in the least measure[2].

Ideas for exploration:

1. Amnesty international supports prisoners of conscience, those who speak out what they see as truth, non-violently. Would Jesus today be a prisoner of conscience?

2. What do Christians need to do in order to ensure that they are committed to developing, with others, a 'Culture of Tolerance and a Life of Truthfulness'?

---

1. W. Wink, *Engaging the Powers*, p. 140
2. Thomas Helwys, *The Mystery of Iniquity*, p.3

At the 1893 World Parliament of Religions, Swami Vivekananda claimed that all religions are true.

One should speak the truth and speak it pleasingly; should not speak the truth in an unpleasant manner nor should one speak untruth because it is pleasing; this is the eternal law.

Manu Smriti, 4.138

It is always proper to speak the truth. It is better again to speak what is beneficial than to speak what is true. I hold that this is truth which is fraught with the greatest benefit to all creatures.

Mahabharata, Shanti Parva 329.13

No matter by what path men approach me, they are made welcome. For all paths, no matter how diverse, lead straight to me. All paths are mine, notwithstanding by what names they may be called.

Bhagavad Gita., 4.11

A HINDU VIEW OF COMMITMENT TO A CULTURE OF TOLERANCE AND A LIFE OF TRUTHFULNESS

The history of Hindu thought clearly shows that thousands of years ago Hindus agreed to disagree over what the ultimate truth is. Thus, Hinduism is not based on belief in one central God, one divine scripture received from that divine entity, or a binding set of principles as enunciated by a particular divine representative on earth.

The result of that has been an inherent tolerance of Hindus towards differences among themselves as well as to adherents of other faiths and cultures. If one cannot define properly who is a Hindu and who is not, one cannot argue over truth, only truthfulness. Sanskrit, the classical Indian language, clearly distinguishes between the word for universal order or truth (*rita*) and any form of more or less subjective truth (*satya*). The universal order is not a matter of acceptance or belief, because it exists whether we believe or accept it or not. As for relations between people, however, the values of tolerance and truthfulness demand of individuals that they respect 'the other', speak the truth, and act in solidarity.

The resulting flexibility of Hindu responses to anything controversial sometimes disturbs outsiders. It also allows them to argue that Hindus are the most intolerant people in the world, given the excesses of the caste system and other divisive structures. Hindus would respond that the tolerance of differences is in itself a valuable ethical foundation and that, as a result, it is more truthful to try to live with the inevitable differences, and to iron out abuses, than to pretend that everyone is equal when this is patently not so.

Words of Swami Vivekananda at the 1893 World's Parliament of Religions:

I am proud to belong to a religion which has taught the world both tolerance and universal acceptance. We believe not only in universal toleration, but we accept all religions as true. I am proud to belong to a nation which has sheltered the persecuted and the refugees of all religions and all nations of the earth.

Question

Do you agree that all religions are true?

A JEWISH VIEW OF COMMITMENT TO A CULTURE OF TOLERANCE AND A LIFE OF TRUTHFULNESS

While tolerance might be seen as a pretty limited value, it would be no bad thing if we could approximate to it! Similarly, truthfulness, on the basis of 'applauding virtue and condemning sin', obviously deserves a strong vote. However, tact and diplomacy also have a part to play and sometimes 'telling it like it is' might lead 'truthfulness' to conflict with 'tolerance'. The example given of scientists not lending their skills and authority to 'questionable' causes is fine, but no doubt many in the past have lent their support to what turned out subsequently to be 'questionable' but at the time seemed most laudable – eugenics is an obvious case in point. Similarly, there must be some cults or practices that one considers entirely beyond the pale. Is it tolerance or truthfulness that takes the lead in responding?

A culture of tolerance and a commitment to truthfulness may not always sit easily together. According to the Rabbis, even God found that sometimes truthfulness had to be subordinated to the needs of tolerance.

The Rabbis make one of the highest values what they call 'Shalom bayit' (household peace) and they used an example from the Torah to illustrate God's suppression of the truth to maintain it. In Genesis (18: 12–13), Sarah, wife of Abraham overhears the prophecy that she will bear a child. She laughs to herself and says, 'Can I possibly bear a child now that I am too old and my husband is old also'. And God says to Abraham: 'Why did Sarah laugh saying that she was too old to bear a child? Is anything impossible for God?' They note that God does not pass on Sarah's negative comment about Abraham. There is, they say, no benefit in total honesty in domestic life. One must be sensitive to the feelings of others and maintain domestic harmony by that kind of sensitivity even at the cost of truthfulness.

In the Midrash, the rabbis tell another story, appearing to applaud lack of truthfulness for a higher purpose – the promotion of goodwill and peace. They tell of the tradition that Aaron, the first High Priest, brother of Moses, promoted peace between people by going first to one and then to the other of two people who had fallen out, and telling each of them in turn, 'If only you knew how upset your fellow is that you have argued!' When the two met again, they frequently made up, believing the other to be desirous of a reconciliation.

You may modify a statement in the interests of peace.

Talmud, Yebamot 65b

In Jewish tradition only two things are called 'True'. God is described sometimes as 'True' and the text of the Torah, the core sacred scripture of the Jewish tradition. The Hebrew word for 'True' is 'Emet', in Hebrew a three letter word, consisting of the first, the middle and the last letter of the alphabet. The Rabbis comment that 'Truth comprehends everything in the world, but, of course, we can only perceive aspects of it at any one time'. As a result we must be wary of thinking that we have a monopoly on the truth.

Because of this attitude, it is more than possible for two people to disagree and yet both be right. Furthermore, truth is something bigger than mere factuality. Accepting that the Biblical account of the creation is 'true' does not also imply that it is factually accurate. For this reason, Jewish tradition didn't falter when Darwin promulgated his Theory of Evolution. It was not necessary to deny a scientific theory just because it didn't concur exactly with the Torah text. They were simply expressing two different ways of looking at things. This has resulted in a very free and active intellectual life for Jews, allowing a wide diversity of ways of looking at things, beause of the impossibility of anyone having a monopoly on truth, even when considering something as 'true' as God or the Torah.

In this Jews have something useful to offer the world. In general, Jews have little interest in arriving at the 'Truth' as between different religious groups. Largely, Jews do not much care what others believe and accept that agreeing to differ might be the best way to get along. The critical thing is right behaviour and so long as people behave well, their understanding of what is 'True' is hardly of interest. This reflects the fact that Jews tend to be rather less 'doctrine-driven', though it must be said that there is a modern trend to become much more concerned with 'right-believing' between Jews – something which has not much bothered them until the 20th century.

Thus, if one had to choose between the two values of tolerance and truthfulness, it would seem that there is a Jewish preference for tolerance, since Truth is so often unknowable. Having said that, there appears to be no uncertainty that Truth is not merely a relative thing that doesn't really exist except in the mind of each person. Rather, there is Truth but it is so great that each of us can only ever have an inkling of a part of it.

However, there is a level where truth has a more domestic and immediate meaning. Here we are not talking about 'Absolute Truths' but ordinary probity and honesty. Here, Judaism is uncompromising. It is wrong

Run to and fro through the streets of Jerusalem,
look and take note!
Search her squares to see
if you can find a man,
one who does justice
and seeks truth;
that I may pardon her . . .
O Lord, do not thy eyes look for truth?

Jeremiah 5.1–3

When man appears before the Throne of Judgment, the first question he is asked is not, "Have you believed in God,"or "Have you prayed and performed ritual acts," but "Have you dealt honourably, faithfully in all your dealings with your fellow man?"

Talmud, Shabbat 31a

The seal of God is truth.
Talmud, Shabbat 55

to mislead anyone by misrepresentation of the facts. Extending the idea from the prohibition in the Torah not to 'put a stumbling block before the blind', the rabbis teach that, for example, a merchant must make known the weaknesses of a product, must not decorate something being sold so that its true nature or quality is no longer evident, that perjury is a very serious offence and so on. Put simply, while they do not believe one should be too insistent on 'Truth', 'factuality' is a very different thing and the stating of facts should be clear and unequivocal.

Questions for discussion

1. Looking at the front page of today's newspaper, how would you divide the material as between facts and opinions? How many of those opinions are posing as facts?

2. In a discussion with others, discover whether or not there is anything which you can agree is 'True', which is not merely factual.

3. By examining two religions, identify ways on which they fundamentally disagree on the 'Truth'.

4. Is tolerance a virtue, or is it a minimum standard?

5. Identify ways in which truthfulness is relevant as a moral principle in your local shopping centre.

6. Modern relationship therapy urges honesty between partners as a way of ensuring that they both understand one another. God, in His exchange with Abraham and Sarah, appears to disagree. What do you think is the balance between honesty and tact?

7. Jews appear to be more tolerant of others disagreeing with them than of disagreements between themselves. Can you think of other situations in which this pattern of behaviour is evident and do you think it is natural/ unacceptable/preferable?

A MUSLIM VIEW OF COMMITMENT TO A CULTURE OF TOLERANCE AND A LIFE OF TRUTHFULNESS

Fulfil the covenant of God once you have pledged it, and do not break any oaths once they have been sworn to. You have set up God as a Guarantee for yourselves; God knows everything you are doing.

Do not be like a woman who unravels her yarn after its strands are firmly spun. Nor take your oaths in order to snatch at advantages over one another, to make one party more numerous than the other. For God will test you by this.

Qur'an 16.91-92

O mankind! behold, we have created you all out of a male and female, and have made you into nations and tribes, so that you might come to know one another. Verily, the noblest among you in the sight of God is the one who is most deeply conscious of Him.

Qur'an 49:13

If God had so willed, He could surely have made you all one single community; but (He willed otherwise) to test you by means of what He has vouchsafed unto you. Vie, then with one another in doing good works. Unto God you must all return; and then He will make you truly understand all that on which you were wont to differ.

Qur'an 5:48

What about truthfulness and tolerance? The Qur'an tells us 'Be ever steadfast in upholding equity, bearing witness to truth for the sake of God, even though it be against your own selves or parents or kinsfolk. Whether the person concerned be rich or poor, God's claim takes precedence over (the claims of) either of them. Do not follow your own desires, lest you swerve from justice; for if you distort the truth behold God is indeed aware of all that you do.' (Qur'an 4. 135)

There is no doubt that telling the truth is incumbent upon all of us and I do not want to discuss it further. You might like to discuss how deceit erodes friendship, family and public life.

Tolerance has many meanings. Colloquially to tolerate something often means putting up with something with bad grace. Tolerance also means not being provoked or being self-righteous. One illustration is from the life of the Prophet. He used to pass regularly one of his neighbours houses and each time the woman of the house would empty her dust and rubbish over him. One day this did not happen. The Prophet found out that she was ill and went to visit her to see how she was and if she needed anything. She was moved by the Prophet's kindness and desisted thenceforth from her provocative behaviour. Later she converted to Islam. It is easy to be tolerant of those we like. A true test of tolerance is to be patient and forgiving of those we dislike.

> **Question**
>
> Why to you think dishonesty and deceit erodes family life, friendship and public life?
>
> Speaking or writing with rudeness and contempt about another person's faith can cause deep offence and may even lead to violence. There are laws in some countries against stirring up racial hatred. Do you think there should also be laws against provoking religious hatred?

A RASTAFARIAN VIEW OF COMMITMENT TO A CULTURE OF TOLERANCE AND A LIFE OF TRUTHFULNESS

A culture of tolerance is something that I, as a Rastafarian, am unable to identify with, because taken together with other coded language such as 'authentically human' and 'fully human', the term 'tolerance' may presuppose an hierarchical structure of culture and races. Many Rastafarians would find an alternative term such as 'a culture of respect' to be more appropriate and acceptable. Religious doctrines and systems cannot be understood in a vacuum or in isolation from the social, political, cultural, anthropological and historical environments that produce them. In this regard the Rastafarian doctrine grew out of the realities of the African peoples over the past 500 years and represents a Pan-African renaissance of human worth and self-dignity in the face of slavery, brutality, discrimination, abuse, exploitation colonial and neo-colonial domination. There is no missionising in Rastafarian doctrine. One is born a Rasta, and there is no process of evangelising or conversion. One becomes aware of divine status by the removal of the effects of Western brainwashing, distortions, lies, half truths, stereotyped self images and propaganda, which cloud our inner vision of Jah (who is love). With such a foundation it is not surprising that Rastafarian doctrine has an ethos of respect for others.

The apparent missionising ethos of the Global Ethic raises another concern. How can we be absolute about truth? The distinction between 'truth' and 'truthfulness' is not made clear. This in turn poses a further question: whose truth does the 'Global Ethic' address? The lack of clarity as to the meaning of 'truth' and 'truthfulness', and the coded language in the text appears to veil a Western hegemonic agenda. For many Rastas this will be particularly worrying, given the traditional role of many Western oriented Churches in the Caribbean in conveying false images and stereotypes concerning the movement. In the Bahamas, the visit of Bob Marley for a charitable concert for the International Year of the Child, provoked an unprecedented outcry against the Rastafarian community by prominent Christian theologians, who actively engaged in 'Rasta bashing' and created a number of negative, false images of Rastafarians. For some this position exposed the hypocrisy of many 'Christians' who neglected to make any contribution to the International Year of the Child or to address many of the pressing social issues affecting Bahamian youth. Western religion is seen by many Rastas to be at the core of socialisation of Black people towards tolerance of colonial and neo-colonial domination.

For many Rastas, truth is revealed by constant study of the Bible and history, dialectical reasoning and most importantly by living according to the laws of our true natures.

In Rastafarian doctrine there is constant debate and reasoning as to what constitutes 'truth'. This is reflected in the Rasta view of politics. For most Rastafarians politics is an inherently dishonest exercise, which has led to it being re-designated as 'poly-tricks', and democracy as 'demonocracy'. This had led to the majority of Rastas boycotting the electoral process. Some point out that in school when work is evaluated by teachers, an incorrect answer is marked with an 'X' to signify that it is wrong. For this reason it is wrong to vote in elections, as this entails the marking of an 'X' on the ballot. However some Rastas, invoking the argument that liberation must be achieved by any means necessary, have become actively involved in the political process. In Jamaica, Rasta Sam Brown has become a veteran political candidate in elections, albeit an unsuccessful one, and he has helped to raise some important Rastafarian concerns in the Jamaican political realm. Similarly many Rastas actively supported and voted for the former Prime Minister, Michael Manley.

Even the prophet Marcus Mosiah Garvey himself ran as a candidate in local parish council elections in Jamaica. Perhaps the fact that his opponent, a member of the white ruling class of the time, won the seat has much to do with the overall Rastafarian aversion to the electoral process.

Another debate currently taking place in the Rastafarian community is to be found in the principle of repatriation. Although most Rastafarians will, without hesitation, assert that 'physical repatriation to Africa is a must!'; there are some who have contended that repatriation does not mean physical movement to Africa, but is rather a spiritual or mental concept. Similarly there is ongoing dynamic discussion about the role of Rastas in the broader African liberation struggle, and more relevant to our present discussion, whether the movement should be involved in initiatives such as the Parliament of World Religions and the Global Ethic Declaration. This reveals that truth is often a dynamic concept that must be viewed in the context of time, space and self. The result of these realities, is that for many Rastas there are more questions than answers and the more we find out the less we know. However it is only by living in accordance with our true natures that we are able to arrive at 'self-truth'. For most Rastas it is important to understand 'self', which in turn provides a guide or compass for correct living. It has been pointed out that, in the Kamitic tradition, self knowledge is the beginning and end of all knowledge. Truth is not partial and once revealed to us, we are obligated to live it, no matter how unpleasant it may be.

In the context of the Global Ethic, there must be a recognition that each religion has its own truth. In coming together to confront the many problems that plague humankind, we must move away from a rhetorical truth and adopt inner reflection on an individual basis, as well in the collective framework of our respective religions and doctrines. This involves a search for inner truth based on a reassessment of each religion in its historical context. For many Western based religions, doctrines, theologians and philosophers this will no doubt be a painful and difficult process. Nevertheless it is a prerequisite for the healing of the deep psychological wounds that divide East and West and North and South. Any dialogue in the framework of a Global Ethic must allow not only for diversity, but also mutual respect, devoid of any taint of racial, cultural or other form of superiority. Religions are bound to disagree over truths and we should agree to disagree, thereby providing room for plurality. The adoption of an inward-looking search for self-truth would avert the taint of an outward looking missionising and evangelising exercise by the Global Ethic. As the old adage goes: To thine own self be true, for the truth shall set you free!

A SIKH VIEW OF COMMITMENT TO A CULTURE OF TOLERANCE AND A LIFE OF TRUTHFULNESS

One God

Truth is the name

Creator

Without fear

Without Hate

Immortal

Is neither born nor dies

Revealed by the grace of the Guru

Meditate!

Truth in the beginning

Truth during the ages

Truth now

Truth shall ever be.

Japji Sahib verse 1: GGS-1

The truth is the remedy for all, washes away all sins

Nanak prays that faith be his wrap.

Guru Nanak: Asa Di Var – Verse 10

The Golden temple at Amristsar, a symbol of openness and worship to people coming from all directions.

Sikhs believe that the second name of the divine is truth. In the first verse of Sri Guru Granth Sahib, the Sikh scriptures, when God is described, Truth is mentioned five times as the name of God. It is very significant that Truth and God are as one and the same in the Sikh faith and therefore it is essential for us to lead a life of honesty and truth.

However there is a lot of deceit and untruthfulness around us. It can be seen in our political systems, sometimes in religious leadership and in the media. Religious fanaticism and intolerance is increasing towards those who are different. Sikh men and women can be subjected to discrimination because they are much easier to identify because of the symbols and turbans (mainly worn by men). The flames of racism are fanned mostly through the vehicle of lies.

Some say Rama, Rama

Some say Khudai

Some worship Gosain

Some Worship Allah

Some call Creator

Some Call Maker

Some call Compassionate

Some Benevolent

Some Bathe in the Sacred Rivers

Some go to do Hajj

Some Worship, some bow

Some read the Vedas

Some read the Qur'an

Some wear blue

Some wear white

Some call themselves Turks (Muslims)

Some call themselves Hindu

Some are after Heaven

Some are after the place of the gods

Nanak says the one who accepted God's command

Is the one who understands the mystery of God

GGS-885

One Parent

We are all children of that one parent

to God? Why?

GGS-611

The Sikh faith believes that there are many paths to the divine and they respect the ways of people of other faiths. In one hymn beginning *'Some say Rama'*, there is a clear reference to how different people and faith groups refer to God in different ways. Worship is also different, but there is a unity of faith.

At the time that this hymn was composed there were two main religions in India, Islam and Hinduism though there are references to Buddhism and Jainism in the holy book. There were also many religious sects amongst the Hindus. The Guru wished people to recognise there are many different ways to God.

Therefore there is in Sikhism a willing acceptance of other faiths and as a result, very little missionizing, except within the faith.

Sikhism encourages young people as far as it is possible to think, speak and act truthfully. In the Sikh tradition it is important that they see, hear, and feel the truth and not accept facts covered in a variety of veils. Truth and trust go hand in hand.

Questions

Why is truthfulness given importance in Sikhism?

Why Does Sikhism accept other faiths as paths to God?

Do you think truthfulness is important in public life? Who is responsible for upholding standards of integrity? Judges, Religious Leaders, Politicians, Members of the Media?

Why do you think some groups of people are the victims of intolerance and discrimination? What is the most helpful way for them to respond to such treatment?

A ZOROASTRIAN VIEW OF COMMITMENT TO A CULTURE OF TOLERANCE AND LIFE OF TRUTHFULNESS

In truth, the liars would threaten us with their evil actions, since they would bring with themselves death and destruction upon people. The strong ones will always bring oppression upon the meeker ones. They do not care for Thy Sacred Law, i.e. The Law of Asha, O Mazda, because they always remain at a distance from truth and Vohuman remains afar from them.

The sage, being aware that love and faith towards God are actual sources of truth, shall teach those who have gone astray and evil persons the way to train their minds with good thoughts, perform good actions and love others. Ultimately, all wicked persons, by learning the truth, shall come towards Thee, O Mazda Ahura.

GY 34,8 & 10

We yearn for Thy mighty light which is shining through truth, O Lord of Life.

GY 34,4

The teachings of Zoroaster on the issue of truthfulness stand at the core of the religion. The centrality of the tenet of following the path of **asha** should be apparent from the regular references to the principle of righteousness, represented by light and therefore the sun or fire. Zoroastrians are told that to lie is to take the opposite path to that of **asha.** Lying is impurity of thought, word and deed and is condemned alongside dishonesty as taking the path of bad thought, **angra maniyo,** which in later Zoroastrian texts comes to be thought of as the evil spirit or energy.

Dishonesty is thus a manifestation of impurity and from early childhood, infants are told that it is unZoroastrian to lie, a contrast being implicitly made with those who are not Zoroastrian. Negative attributes aligned with lying are dirtiness, darkness, infertile or swampy land, and at the opposite pole truthfulness is categorised with accompanying concepts such as light, fire, whiteness, cleanliness and cultivation. For this reason some Western scholars have called Zoroastrianism an *ethical dualism*

As a result of this inculcation from childhood, Zoroastrians have acquired a reputation amongst those who have had dealings with them as a community of people whose words and deeds can be trusted. Both in Iran and in India they are marked out as people who are known to be honest and who will neither exploit nor cheat. Some Zoroastrians themselves point out that this may be the result of centuries of persecution during which they were always the underdog and in a minority. In such a position they would be even more vulnerable if they did not deal honestly with those in greater power than themselves. However, it is nevertheless the case that two Greek writers, (and therefore theoretically their political enemies) Herodotus and Xenophon, both single out the ancient Iranians who were Zoroastrian for their upbringing of great integrity and honesty.

It is true that if a society is to function with harmony and with concord, there has to be trust between people. Trust comes from knowing that people operate with a conscience and act honestly. The concept of trust was enshrined in the spirit of **mehr** or **Mitra,** represented by the symbol of purity, the sun or fire. **Mitra** has a prominent role in Zoroastrianism and temples are informally known in Iran as the Doors of Mithra. The

The wicked persons, O Mazda, who turn away from Thy Holy Spirit, they feel themselves ever-thwarted, but no truthful man shall ever act like that. The truthful person, though of small possessions and poor should be loved and respected, but followers of untruth, though of great possessions and power should be despised and regarded as wicked.

GY 47,4

cult of Mithraism was taken up by the Romans who came into contact with late Zoroastrian ideas and they spread it as far as Britain, albeit with very different associations.

The spirit of tolerance pervades Zoroastrian teaching. It relies very much on the idea that every person has the innate ability to hear the voice of *conscience*, and with an unclouded mind and in a balanced and well-functioning society, each individual should be able to discern the right path for him/herself. For this reason as mentioned above, a Zoroastrian will not perform a violent or aggressive act by trying to force a person round to his/her point of view, but will rely on common sense to prevail and free choice to take place. It is not acceptable to a Zoroastrian that an idea should be forced upon someone who is not ready to accept it of their own free will, even if it is sincerely believed that it will be better for the other person. To use force is to show a lack of respect.

During the time of the three great Persian empires, up till the advent of Islam, the surviving records of the attitudes and deeds of the Persian kings suggests that they were true to the teachings of their Zoroastrian faith and did not force their subject people to abandon their own faiths. There are however, a few exceptions to this tradition in the later period and they are to be regretted. Indeed the Old Testament even records how one of the Zoroastrian kings freed the Jews and helped them to rebuild their temple in Jerusalem.

With the centuries of persecution already alluded to, this non-evangelical stance was a safe position for Zoroastrians to take as any attempt to persuade another to change faith would result in execution for both. This stance has become interpreted over the centuries by Zoroastrians themselves as one which denies the right of others to accept Zoroastrian ideas and to call themselves Zoroastrian. It is today being challenged and re-examined as it is intolerance reversed and therefore not true to Zoroastrianism!

The Zoroastrian threshold of tolerance is being tested from within the community as the two communities, Iranian and Indian, separated over centuries have evolved into significantly different ways. Each claims greater fidelity and authenticity to the old ways and takes up a different position on matters such as intermarriage, conversion and acceptance.

Each of these claims to greater fidelity or authenticity to the 'true tradition' are respectively reflective of cultural differences.

The Fourth Directive is:

Commitment to a culture of equal rights and partnership between men and women

A BAHA'I VIEW OF COMMITMENT TO A CULTURE OF EQUAL RIGHTS AND PARTNERSHIP BETWEEN MEN AND WOMEN

In the vegetable world there are male plants and female plants; they have equal rights, and possess an equal share of the beauty of their species; though indeed the tree that bears fruit might be said to be superior to that which is unfruitful.

In the animal kingdom we see that the male and the female have equal rights; and that they each share the advantages of their kind.

'Abdu'l-Baha, *Paris Talks* 160-1

In some respects woman is superior to man. She is more tender-hearted, more receptive, her intuition is more intense.

'Abdu'l-Baha, *Paris Talks* 161

In the Writings of the Baha'i Faith the matter of equality is one of basic and natural justice. All peoples, no matter what race, sex, nationality, or situation are regarded equally, and are assured of full human rights.

Historically, civilizations and religions have tended to deny full rights to women, so this is addressed fully in the Baha'i Faith. The Prophet Baha'u'llah clearly announced the principle of the equality of women and men as a Divine Truth.

In many places in the Baha'i Writings an analogy is made between the different levels of existence, making the point that equality exists between the sexes in the other kingdoms. In the world of humanity, however, men have claimed superiority and great differences have been allowed to develop. Women have often not been permitted to claim equal rights – but this is contrary to natural justice and Divine law.

> *'Baha'u'llah emphasized and established the equality of man and woman. Sex is not particularized to humanity; it exists throughout the animate kingdoms but without distinction or preference. In the vegetable kingdom there is complete equality between male and female of species. Likewise in the animal plane equality exists; all are under the protection of God. Is it becoming to man that he, the noblest of creatures, should observe and insist upon such distinction?* ('Abdu'l-Baha, *Baha'i World Faith* 24)

The reason it has appeared over the ages that women are inferior is the fact that women have been denied education which would show that they are as equally capable as men. As soon as women everywhere are given full opportunities it will be clear that both sexes are equally able to achieve.

The achievement of an equal balance in humanity is not only desirable, but imperative for the well-being of society, its stability, and progress.

> *'The happiness of mankind will be realized when women and men co-ordinate and advance equally, for each is the complement and helpmeet of the other.'* ('Abdu'l-Baha, *Baha'i World Faith* 241)

If the mother is educated then her children will be well taught. When the mother is wise, then will the children be led into the path of wisdom.

It is clear therefore that the future generation depends on the mothers of today.

Divine Justice demands that the rights of both sexes should be equally respected since neither is superior to the other in the eyes of Heaven. Dignity before God depends not on sex, but on purity and luminosity of heart. Human virtues belong equally to all!

'Abdu'l-Baha, *Paris Talks* 162

Women have equal rights with men ... As long as women are prevented from attaining their highest possibilities, so long will men be unable to achieve the greatness which might be theirs.

'Abdu'l-Baha, *Paris Talks* 133

'In this Revelation of Baha'u'llah, the women go neck and neck with the men. In no movement will they be left behind. Their rights with men are equal in degree. They will enter all the administrative branches of politics. They will attain in all such a degree as will be considered the very highest station of the world of humanity and will take part in all affairs.' ('Abdu'l-Baha, *Paris Talks* 182)

Think about the long-term results for the world when all women are fully educated and have the freedom to fulfil their potential.

- ? How will children benefit?
- ? How will men benefit?
- ? How will the human race benefit?
- ? Why should men work to change past inequalities and now encourage women to achieve fully?

Keywords

Balance   *Justice*   *Education*

'The world of humanity has two wings – one is women and the other men. Not until both wings are equally developed can the bird fly. Should one wing remain weak, flight is impossible. Not until the world of women becomes equal to the world of men in the acquisition of virtues and perfections, can success and prosperity be attained as they ought to be.'

('Abdu'l-Baha, *Faith for Everyman* 63)

A BRAHMA KUMARIS VIEW OF COMMITMENT TO A CULTURE OF EQUAL RIGHTS AND PARTNERSHIP BETWEEN MEN AND WOMEN

The basis of real love between people is spiritual. To see another as a spiritual being, a soul, is to see the spiritual reality of the other. To be conscious of that reality is to have spiritual love; each person, complete within, independent yet totally connected, recognises that state in the other. As a result, there is a constant and natural love. True love is when the soul has love for the soul. Love of the soul is eternal; the soul never dies. Such love is righteous, and it brings joy. Attachment to that which is perishable is unrighteous, and it brings sorrow.

Living Values

A Vision of Equality

Inequality between men and women exists in communities around the world. It is a fundamental inequality at the heart of society's main unit of the family. However, within the Brahma Kumaris teachings is the concept of an original state of human society where equality and partnership are the norm. In order to recreate such a state of affairs, many values, systems and traditions of the world have to be challenged.

A Challenge to the World

Brahma Baba, the Founder of the Brahma Kumaris, issued such a challenge in a very practical way. In establishing the University in 1936, he asked 12 young women in their late teens and early twenties to become the trustees of the wealth that he had accumulated during his life. This was quite a revolution for the traditional community in which he lived. Over the next 33 years, Brahma Baba then patiently and diligently empowered those women to become spiritual leaders. Today, those women, now known as Dadis (elder sisters) head a Spiritual University of over 400,000 regular students throughout 77 countries, with outreach programmes involving hundreds of thousands of people around the world.

The aim of such a system, where women play the leading administrative roles for students of both sexes, is to redress the imbalance of centuries and to facilitate the balanced development of both the masculine and feminine qualities that are within each and every individual, regardless of gender. Real partnership based on equality then becomes possible.

Equality of Vision

To develop such partnership, there has to be a vision of equality that goes beyond gender. The only way that this is possible is through 'soul consciousness' or the awareness that I am a soul, a child of God, and all others that I interact with are also souls. Without this awareness, we see others only in terms of gender and we can fall into the old patterns of action of oppression and submission between the sexes that have caused so much unhappiness. The soul is a being of light, very different in nature to the body. The soul is eternal; the body has a limited life span. Soul awareness enables me to have a constant vision of the inner qualities of myself and of those I interact with. Expressing values such as respect, tolerance and acceptance is then naturally part of my behaviour.

Balanced Expression

The human soul, the living being or self that functions through the costume of the body, is, in its original form, a perfect being. In the section, 'What it means to be fully human', the original qualities of the soul were described as love, peace, happiness, wisdom and strength. In the perfect being, the outer expression of each of these qualities creates a positive state of virtue in the male and female. The qualities that are usually described as feminine, for example, care, nurture and compassion, are also equally expressed by men. Qualities that are usually described as masculine, decision taking, leadership, courage, are also equally expressed by women. Thus partnership becomes possible, and love becomes the foundation for all interaction.

The Effect on Family Life

A family of partnership is a family of respect, harmony and joy. It is a family where everyone is respected and valued, whether young or old, talented or less talented, achieving or less achieving. In such a family everyone is listened to and included in decision-making and shared responsibility. Such family life also ensures the balanced development of the children in an environment where spiritual and moral values are naturally lived.

> - Make a list of the characteristics of a relationship based on true partnership. To what extent can I see these characteristics expressed in my own relationships?
>
> - What is the foundation of a true vision of equality? Can I practise this today with someone close to me?

A BUDDHIST VIEW OF COMMITMENT TO A CULTURE OF EQUAL RIGHTS AND PARTNERSHIP BETWEEN MEN AND WOMEN

Brethren, one can never repay two persons, I declare. What two? Mother and Father.

Even if one could carry about his mother on one shoulder and his father on the other, and so doing should live a hundred years; and if he should support them, anointing them with unguents, kneading and rubbing their limbs, and they meanwhile should even void their excrements upon him – even so he could not repay his parents. Moreover, if he should establish his parents in supreme authority, in the absolute rule over this mighty earth abounding in the seven treasures – not even thus could he repay his parents. Why not? Brethren, parents do much for their children; they bring them up, they nourish them, they introduce them to this world.

However, brethren, whoso incites his unbelieving parents, settles and establishes them in the faith; whoso incites his immoral parents, settles and establishes them in morality; whoso incites his stingy parents, settles and establishes them in liberality; whoso incites his foolish parents, settles and establishes them in wisdom – such a one, just by doing, does repay, does more than repay what is due to his parents.

Buddhism. Anguttara Nikaya i.61

Are the differences between the lives of men and women just a matter of social convention, or do we have different natures ?

In theory, Buddhism has always been clear that our fundamental (buddha) nature is one and indivisible. It has existed through countless lives. It must be beyond differences like male/female, black/white, clever/stupid. The same dharma is offered to all living beings, because they all have this same nature.

'What was your original face; the one you had before your mother and father conceived you ? '

(If you stop reading and look, you can see this face, now.)

This is not to deny that male and female exist. Sexual difference and desire are not repressed but seen as energies to be transformed. Boddhisattvas ("saints") have often been pictured as androgynous – having the physical features of man and woman in one body. Or they are imagined as embracing couples. The spiritual path involves understanding, uniting and transcending the male and female aspects of our nature.

The Buddha in his lifetime created a spiritual order for men and one for women. His wife and aunt were among the first nuns. But this order of nuns was allowed to die out in some countries after a time, only men being ordained. The patriarchal assumptions of culture bent the gender partnership in an unequal direction, so that where there are nuns they have often been treated as inferiors, even servants of the monks. The idea of rebirth has been used as a justification for this; women might be men in the next life – so don't complain ! This inequality is much more marked in some traditions of Buddhism than others, showing that it is only a matter of social prejudice. As women in Asian societies have become more assertive and as western trained Buddhists increase in numbers, these practices are being challenged and are changing. The Dalai Lama has promised to raise the unequal position of women at the highest level in the Tibetan traditions. In the West, many women Buddhist teachers have now been trained and have many students of both sexes.

In traditional Buddhist countries, monks have often been 'given' by their family to the monastery at a young age. They may be unsure about their commitment to maintaining celibacy, especially when tempted by the freer atmosphere in Western countries. This has led to sexual scandals involving Asian teachers and western students, where the students have felt exploited. This has caused a questioning of the idea, which has existed in some schools, of submitting completely to the teacher.

All this is part of the process of separating the essential Buddhist teachings from the cultural packaging which history has added to them, with all its biases including an undervaluing of women's spirituality. If the Buddha's teachings are universal, they can exist perfectly well with modern social conditions and do not need to preserve gender assumptions from past centuries, any more than we need to retain ancient ideas about geography or the origin of the universe. Buddhism is free to change in this way because it is a method of spiritual development, not a set of eternal answers.

Question

Do you think inequalities between men and women are only because of social convention and prejudice?

Do you think the teachings of some religions contribute to that inequality?

A CHRISTIAN VIEW OF COMMITMENT TO A CULTURE OF EQUAL RIGHTS AND PARTNERSHIP BETWEEN MEN AND WOMEN.

You shall not commit adultery.
Exodus 20:16

When Adam delved and Eve span, who was then the gentleman?

John Ball, 1381

Impurity in the sexual sphere consists in using another person solely in order to satisfy desire. It is there wherever people enter into sexual intimacy with no intention of forming a lasting bond. The starkest form of impurity occurs when a person engages in sexual intercourse for the sake of money... Impurity is not only related to sex: a person defiles his heart if he knows his neighbour is hungry but goes to bed without giving him food.

J.C. Arnold *A Plea for Purity – Sex, Marriage and God*, p.39 and p.43

Christians are ambiguous about the place of women. Genesis begins with male and female created equally in the image of God (Genesis 1:27) but then comes the fall and Eve is told 'yet your desire shall be for your husband, and he shall rule over you.' (Genesis 3:16) Paul in the New Testament argued on the one hand that 'it is shameful for a woman to speak in church' and on the other that in Christ 'there is neither male nor female' (1 Corinthians 14:35, Galatians 3:28)

Jesus though is different. Even before he was born, his pregnant mother Mary on meeting her cousin, Elizabeth, boldly exclaimed:

My soul magnifies the Lord,
and my spirit rejoices in God my Saviour,
for he has regarded the low estate of his handmaiden...
he has put down the mighty from their thrones,
and exalted those of low degree;
he has filled the hungry with good things,
and the rich he has sent empty away.
(Luke 1:46-48, 52–3)

Jesus' own encounters with women are different. He prevented the woman caught in adultery from being stoned (John 8:1–11); he talked with the woman at the well who had had five husbands and was currently living with another man (John 4:5–30); he insisted on Mary's right to be a student when her sister Martha wanted her to cook. (Luke 10:38–42) If Eve was the first participant in the fall, the first witness of the resurrection was a woman – Mary Magdalene (John 20:1–18).

Jesus, then and now, challenges male supremacy or patriarchy.

Of even higher status than both men and women are children. The story of Jesus blessing the children is immediately preceded by Jesus' uncompromising teaching on divorce. When asked why Moses permitted divorce Jesus said:

For your hardness of heart he wrote you this commandment. But from the beginning of creation, 'God made them male and female.' For this reason a man shall leave his father and mother and be joined to his wife, and the two shall become one flesh. So they are no longer two but one flesh. What therefore

God has joined together, let not man put asunder. (Mark 10:5-9; cp Matthew 19: 4ff)

There is still much hardness of heart about. And children still remain unblessed as a result.

Allowing women to be priests recently in the Church of England and other churches has been traumatic for many. It remains impossible in the Roman Catholic Church although women's religious orders have been very powerful and the veneration of Mary has raised the status of women. In some churches which teach the 'priesthood of all believers' women have historically enjoyed a higher status with perhaps the Quakers experiencing the most equal partnership between men and women. In the seventeenth century for instance

> ... in their attitude to women the Levellers were ahead of their time. They encouraged women to play their part in politics side with their husbands and brothers, because they believed in the equality of all 'made in the image of God'. This was indeed an article of their religious creed, which reflected the influence of the Anabaptists among them. Everyone knows that however low the position of women sank around them, the Quakers always preached and practised equality. But few of us remember that they were following the example which their forerunners the Anabaptists had set from the early days of the sixteenth century onward. In their community women had an equal standing, an equal right to pray and speak at its meetings. So many of the Levellers were members of this sect that it must have seemed natural to practise on weekdays what they taught on Sundays[1].

Elizabeth Watson, a modern Quaker wrote: 'When I tell young people that I found marriage liberating, they respond, "You've got to be kidding." But it is true. We have kept the goal of being a union of equal comrades, granting each other space to be ourselves and to grow towards wholeness.'[2]

The Scriptures teach us that marriage is a gift of God in creation and a means of his grace, a holy mystery in which man and woman become one flesh. It is God's purpose that, as husband and wife give themselves to each other in love throughout their lives, they shall be united in that love as Christ is united with his Church.

Marriage is given, that husband and wife may comfort and help each other, living faithfully together in need and in plenty, in sorrow and in joy. It is given, that with delight and tenderness they may know each other in love, and, through the joy of their bodily union, may strengthen the union of their hearts and lives. It is given, that they may have children and be blessed in caring for them and bringing them up in accordance with God's will, to his praise and glory.

In marriage husband and wife belong to one another, and they begin a new life together in the community. It is a way of life that all should honour; and it must not be undertaken carelessly, lightly, or selfishly, but reverently, responsibly, and after serious thought.

From the Alternative Marriage Service of the Church of England.

© The Central Board of Finance of the Church of England 1980.

Ideas for exploration:

1. Is the idea of marriage for life old fashioned?
2. Should the welfare of children be the ethical judge of the actions of both men and women?
3. Do male images of God predominate in Christianity ?

---

1. H.N.Brailsford, *The Levellers and the English Reformation*, pp.316-317
2. Yearly Meeting of the Religious Society of Friends [1995] *Quaker Faith and Practice*, 22.38

A HINDU VIEW OF COMMITMENT TO A CULTURE OF EQUAL RIGHTS AND PARTNERSHIP BETWEEN MEN AND WOMEN

The union of hearts and minds and freedom from hate I'll bring you.

Love one another as the cow loves the calf that she has borne.

Let son be loyal to father,

and of one mind with his mother;

Let wife speak to husband words that are honey-sweet and gentle.

Let not a brother hate a brother,

nor a sister hate a sister,

Unanimous, united in aims

speak you words with friendliness.

I will make the prayer for that concord among men at home by which the gods do not separate, nor ever hate one another.

Be not parted – growing old, taking thought, thriving together, moving under a common yoke,

Come speaking sweetly to one another;

I'll make you have one aim and be of one mind. Common be your water-store, common your share of food;

I bind you together to a common yoke.

United, gather round the sacrificial fire like spokes around the nave of a wheel.

With your common desire I'll make you all have one aim, be of one mind, following one leader, like the gods who preserve their immortality.

Morn and eve may there be a loving heart in you.

Atharva Veda 3.30

Hinduism, being focused on diversity and pluralism, assumes that the unity of humankind, in fact of all created beings, is achieved by recognising that there is a collective of individual life forms which are different but all have a share in the created world. For humankind itself, this means that Hinduism views every individual as an entity in his or her own right, not as some uniform but autonomous minute digit. In contrast, the so-called modern Western approach, stipulating that everyone is equal per se, overlooks the fact that people are not actually equal, whether we look at men and women or at social-economic difference.

Hindu culture sees men and women as complementary elements of a larger whole. Being focused on individual obligations, it sees that women inevitably have duties different from men. Only women can bear children, so the men get other jobs in this system of division of labour. Today, this is widely seen as violating international norms of gender justice, but Hindus continue to doubt whether these are in fact international norms, for they seem to be Western cultural constructs imposed on the world as a whole. Hindu culture underwrites the concept of a partnership between man and woman, of 'gender equity' rather than 'gender equality'. Throughout its history, Hindu culture has been focusing on the fluid concept of duties of an individual, depending on his or her position in life, and this continues to be seen as appropriate. Thus, children can expect to be maintained by their parents and will only gradually grow into a position in life where it becomes their duty to maintain others. Grandparents can rely on support mechanisms within the family to support them in their old age, since it is not an element of traditional Hindu culture – nor indeed of modern Indian state law – that the state will provide all sorts of welfare benefits.

The mutual interdependence between husband and wife, parent and child, and others, is clearly not a permanent and stagnant relationship of dependency or superiority, it only looks like this. At any one time, this relationship will change, so that the dominant partner becomes the dependent one.

Making distinctions between men and women, and other unequal partners, thus is not seen as violating some basic ethical norm. Instead, it is perceived as a truthful representation of reality, with which people have to live. While Hinduism as a whole is well familiar with the concept of ultimate universal unity, the acceptance of utter diversity and pluralism is similarly a hallmark of that religious and cultural tradition. This is also reflected in the basic rule that, to achieve justice, one needs to consider the facts and circumstances of any particular case, not some fixed general rule which binds everyone. Obviously, this flies in the face of Western concepts about the rule of law, the power of precedent, and the binding nature of statute laws.

Hinduism has always had much to say on sexual morality. Over time, there have been tremendous changes in basic concepts, but it has always been accepted that without sex there would be no births, and thus no future for humankind. The ancient Hindu concepts of cosmic order put an obligation on men and women to procreate. The few ascetic exceptions confirm the rule and one should not assume that Hinduism is all about monkhood and chastity.

At the basis of Hindu culture, then, remains a clear understanding of the symbiotic nature of the male/female relationship rather than an argument that these two unequal parts are equal in their own right. Both are seen as functioning within the context of the wider cosmic world.

Question

How would you differentiate the concepts of 'gender equity' and 'gender equality'?

He who destroys one human life, the Scripture regards as if he had destroyed the whole world.

The Talmud

We should also pray for the wicked among the peoples of the world; we should love them too. As long as we do not pray in this way, as long as we do not love in this way, the Messiah will not come.

Chasidic Saying

A JEWISH VIEW OF COMMITMENT TO A CULTURE OF EQUAL RIGHTS AND PARTNERSHIP BETWEEN MEN AND WOMEN

Without doubt, and not only because of the terrible experience that Jews have had historically, a commitment to equal rights is high on the Jewish agenda. This is fundamentally underpinned by the principle that all humanity is created in the image of God and therefore deserving of the respect to be accorded to God's 'image'.

The rabbis indicate in various ways this principle, not least being exercised by what can be learnt from the story of Adam in Genesis. They note (in the Midrash, Bereshit Rabbah) that all other creatures were created in numbers at the outset, but that humanity was created in one person initially. They comment that this prevents anyone from arguing that his or her ancestors were greater than someone else's. They also suggest that the earth that God used to create Adam was gathered from around the world, again suggesting that humanity has its origins in every place, thus challenging any attempt at the argument that people from one place are more authentically the 'original' human being.

This idea, that all human beings are descended from the same ancestor, and, by extension, that all human beings are equal in the sight of God, is the belief which underpins the idea of human rights and the equality of humanity. Quite evidently, human beings are not equal, either at birth or as they develop. We are different colours, different sizes, have different capacities and talents, different potentials and preferences. All of this is true even before our upbringing and society aggravates our sense of these differences or intensifies them. However, Jews believe that there is a level on which all of these observable differences do not matter. Put the most wonderful human being next to the most dreadful and, though you cannot see it, they are equal *in the sight of God*, and thus deserving of equal treatment.

However, using the word 'equal' is slightly misleading. The word 'equitable' would be more useful. Jews recognise that there are, both naturally and through social circumstances, inequalities between people. A murderer and a philanthropist should not be treated in an identical way. One should be punished and the other should be honoured. While each has rights, s/he also has responsibilities and each has made choices which result in their different treatment. Such different treatment is as a result of *what they do or have done*. It is not a product of 'who they are'. In that, they are equal human beings.

After the Hebrew Marriage Contract has been read by the Celebrant, the following Seven Benedictions are said:-

Blessed art thou, O Lord our God, King of the universe, who createst the fruit of the vine.

Blessed art thou, O Lord our God. King of the universe, who has created all things to thy glory.

Blessed art thou, O Lord our God, King of the universe, Creator of mankind.

Blessed art thou, O Lord our God, King of the universe, who hast made humanity in thine image, after thy likeness, and has prepared unto him, out of his very self, a perpetual fabric. Blessed art thou, O Lord, Creator of mankind.

May she who was barren (Zion) be exceeding glad and exult, when her children are gathered within her joy. Blessed art thou, O Lord, who makes Zion joyful through her children.

O make these loved companions greatly to rejoice, even as of old thou didst gladden thy creatures in the garden of Eden. Blessed art thou, O Lord, who makest bridegroom and bride to rejoice.

Blessed art thou, O Lord our God, King of the universe, who hast created joy and gladness, bridegroom and bride, mirth and exultation, pleasure and delight, love, brotherhood, peace and fellowship. Soon O Lord, our God, may there be heard in the cities of Judah, and in the streets of Jerusalem, the voice of joy and gladness, the voice of the bridegroom and the voice of the bride, the jubilant voice of bridegrooms from their canopies, and of youths from their feasts of song. Blessed art thou, O Lord, who makest the bridegroom to rejoice with the bride.

Thus it would be stupid in Jewish thought not to allow a blind person to bring his guide dog into a building because there are 'no dogs allowed'. 'Equal' treatment might demand that, but 'equitable' treatment does not. On the other hand, to prevent a black person from going to university just because they're black is utterly unacceptable. Every one deserves equal respect – which may occasionally, to be fair, require differential treatment.

The same principle, applied to people with varying disabilities, of different skin colour, of different religions, applies to men and women. But at this point we enter a debate which is still live in the scientific world and draws different responses from different Jews. No-one is in any doubt that men and women are equal in the sight of God. Each has a right to the same treatment under the law for example, and each must be taken seriously as an independent autonomous human being. There can be no question, for example, of the old European idea of a man 'owning' his wife.

But *if* men and women are naturally *different,* then the principle of 'equity' demands that they should receive differential treatment in order to take that into account. So, for example, *if* women are naturally less aggressive than men (a matter hotly debated in the scientific world) then it would be right to protect women from that aggression or not expect them to be as aggressive as their male counterparts. If it is true that women are more eager to have children and have a family than men (another matter not yet proven but widely believed) then that desire must be accommodated in order to allow women equal treatment with men who, in this view, want children less.

So, while all Jews agree that men and women are of equal value and should be recognised as equal, they differ as to whether men and women function identically and, therefore, whether they should be expected to behave equally. Progressive (Reform and Liberal) Jews tend to the view that men and women should have identical functions and responsibilities, while Orthodox Jews believe men and women have different functions and should act complementarily but not identically.

Here we come to another principle that has to be taken into account when considering this topic. While Judaism accepts the principle of human rights, and it would easily be argued that the Jewish prophets of old were amongst the first people in the world to articulate them, Jews would usually want to set these rights against responsibilities – that might occasionally restrict one's ability to exercise those rights.

Questions for discussion

1. How would you justify believing that all people are equal if you do not believe in one God who created all people equally?

2. Since in Orthodox Jewish tradition, Jewish status is passed on through the mother only, but only men can be rabbis, in your view which sex is considered more important?

3. When might it be better to treat people *equitably* rather than *equally*?

4. According to the Torah, 'strangers' – foreigners – must be treated decently and fairly, 'because you yourselves were strangers in Egypt'. What experiences might you call on to help you remember to treat others as you would like to be treated?

5. 'Love your neighbour as yourself' is a rule from the Torah (Leviticus). Under what circumstances might it be hard in the modern world to live up to that instruction?

6. How far do you think it is true that men and women are intrinsically different? If you think they are, should this make any difference to how they should be treated by society and in law?

7. Is there anything, in your view, that someone can do that leads to them forfeiting their right to equal treatment with other people?

8. If all people are equal and must be treated equally, how can one justify looking after one's family or friends more than one looks after everyone else?

A MUSLIM VIEW OF COMMITMENT TO A CULTURE OF EQUAL RIGHTS AND PARTNERSHIP BETWEEN MEN AND WOMEN

Partnership and equal rights between men and women is really no different from that between all human beings. We are all equal in the eyes of God. He knows us better than we know ourselves. We are different in terms of ability, mental, spiritual and physical strength, aptitude, education, health and wealth. The more we have, the more responsibility we have to use our gifts to the benefit of the less well-endowed.

Although most of what comes within this remit is covered in the paragraphs above, there is the special relationship between husbands and wives. The Holy Qur'an tells us that husbands and wives are partners together. It is difficult to lay down guidelines for such an intimate relationship. In marriage as in all else in life men and women are guided by the principles of justice, charity, truthfulness and kindness. Marriage, and parenthood if it comes, make special demands. The Qur'an says 'And among His wonders is this: He creates for you mates out of your own kind, so that you might incline towards them, and He engenders love and tenderness between you. In this, behold, are messages indeed for people who think.' (Qur'an 30. 21)

Modesty and chaste behaviour is enjoined on men and women. Sexual behaviour outside marriage is forbidden. The husband is responsible for the maintenance of the family. The wife if she wishes and is able may contribute but there is no obligation upon her to do so. It is important to note here that the Qur'an says that what a man earns is his and what a woman earns is hers. All the precepts mentioned above apply to the married couple. Each has a duty to the other to maintain a happy and contented home with each endeavouring to help the other. We know that the Prophet helped his wives with the housework and mended his own clothes and shoes. Wives are asked not to be wasteful since they are managing the family's resources. The Qur'an repeatedly urges people to kindliness, charitable behaviour and to desist from aggression and oppression. The marriage partnership requires all of these together with respect for each other's privacy with regard to the outside world. In general, relationships between men and women are regulated by all the requirements of pious behaviour mentioned above together with the need not to be sexually provocative.

> Unlike most other societies of the time, Islam, from its beginning, recognized women as autonomous legal personalities with civil rights. As a complete legal person the adult Muslim woman is granted title to keep her name forever. She has the right to acquire, keep, and sell property as she pleases in perfect freedom. Her consent must be obtained for any transaction involving her, be it the lease of her property, the cultivation of her field, or, above all, her marriage. She cannot be coerced into anything.
>
> Since woman is not property or an object but a full legal personality, sexual intercourse cannot be a random affair but must be done with the woman's consent and with responsibility, a responsibility that falls on both parties. Sexual promiscuity is vehemently condemned because it is, by definition, a violation of responsibility of one or the other party. That is why Islam counsels its adherents: Have as much sex as you please, but always responsibly.

Isma'il R. Al Faruqui, *Islam*, p.45

Questions

Why does Islam strongly condemn sexual promiscuity?
Why do you think some religions have a high regard for sexuality and others see it in a negative light?

A RASTAFARIAN VIEW OF COMMITMENT TO A CULTURE OF EQUAL RIGHTS AND PARTNERSHIP BETWEEN MEN AND WOMEN

This 'irrevocable directive', for me, as a Rastafarian raises concerns of an underlying Western feminist agenda. Whereas, as mentioned earlier, the Global Ethic does not deal specifically with the issue of Western racial discrimination against Black people and relates the issue to one of inter-racial conflict, it targets gender issues in a Western framework and specifically condemns 'sexual exploitation' and 'sexual discrimination' as one of the worst forms of degradation'.

The Western feminist agenda of the text focuses on issues of 'patriarchy' and this leads us to consider fundamental differences between white and black feminists. It has been argued that historically white leaders of the women's rights movement have neglected issues associated with the Black Movement and the Labour Movement. It has been pointed out that on the whole, and especially since very recently, Western feminist perspectives have paid little attention to the process of racialization of gender, class or sexuality[1].

The use of the term 'patriarchy' has been extensively critiqued by Black feminists, who have asserted that one of the consequences of racism is that Black men do not benefit from patriarchal social structures in the same way as white men and that benefit from patriarchy does not distinguish Black men from Black women.[2] This underscores the ranking of gender over other social phenomena, and the relegation of race to subordinate importance. The emphasis on 'equality' in the Global Ethic is a Western concept and Rastafarians would prefer 'equity' which suggests equilibrium, inter-linkedness, mutual dependency and freedom from malicious deprivation. Most Rastas celebrate the diversity between man and woman, and in the movement women have become increasingly central to most organisational work.

However there is clear recognition of the differences, given the undeniable biological functions of women in respect of procreation and motherhood. Most Rastas are Nazarites, obligated to follow biblical injunctions and prohibition from 'pollution' has to be observed (abstinence from sexual relations or physical contact with a woman during her menstrual cycle). This has most often led to a reversal of perceived sexual roles in a

On the official seal of the Bahamas Law Guild are two conch shells, one male and the other female, balanced by the scales of Bahamian justice, represented by a palm tree.

Western context, with male Rastas usually taking over the domestic duties of the kitchen (something that is imbued in children from an early age). Most Rastafarians will find Western concepts of gender equality to be dishonest and to be part of the overall ethos of 'Babylon' (Western society).

The Rasta ethos is apparent in the official seal of the Bahamas Law Guild, which has two conch shells, one male the other female, balanced by the scales of Bahamian justice (represented by a palm tree). The male conch stands on its base and the female on its side. This emphasizes the diversity of man and woman. Further, the shells are in a state of equilibrium and along with the scales of justice are enveloped by an egg, signifying the essence of creation and unity between man and woman. This position reveals the importance of procreation to the Rastafarian philosophy, a biblical mandate to be fruitful, multiply and replenish the earth. The paramount importance of children, concepts of 'inity' and love ensure that, despite there being diversity and specific roles and duties for the Rasta man and woman, there is no gender exploitation in a Western sense. The Rastafarian woman, rather than being exploited and downgraded, is treated with royal dignity and most often referred to as 'Queen' or 'Princess'.

Questions:

Do you think the Global Ethic reflects the 'Western feminist agenda'?

Why do most Rastafarians regard Western concepts of gender equality as dishonest?

---

1. See Angela Y Davis, *Women, Culture and Politics*, and A. Brah, 'Difference, Diversity and Differentiation' in *Race, Culture and Difference*.
2. See H Carby, 'White Women Listen! Black Feminism and the Boundaries of Sisterhood' in *CCCS: The Empire Strikes Back,* and Caroline Knowles and Sharmila Mercer, 'Feminism and Anti-racism: An exploration of political possibilities' in *Race, Culture and Difference*.

16

A SIKH VIEW OF COMMITMENT TO A CULTURE OF EQUAL RIGHTS AND PARTNERSHIP BETWEEEN MEN AND WOMEN

To you the Lord we pray.

Soul and body are your gifts to us.

You are the Mother, and the Father,

We are your children,

With your grace,

There are countless blessings.

Guru Arjan: Sukhmani Sahib

The Sikhs are shown the way to a truly spiritual marriage, in these words:

They are not husband and wife,

Who merely stay together,

They are,

Who has one light in two bodies.

Guru Armdas: GGS-788.

The Langar, or communal dining, demonstrates the equality of all Sikhs.
Ajit Singh

The spirit of partnership is the key to social ethics in the Sikh faith where men and women are considered equal. In an analogy of human relationships God is described as both mother and father, and is also beyond gender. The Gurus in expressing their relationship to God, chose the feminine gender to describe their love of God.

Sikhs believe in the equality of men and women in faith. There is no priesthood and any Sikh, male or female, who is knowledgeable is able to perform duties of leading the service and performing ceremonies. Sometimes when people of other faiths visit the Gurdwara, they may be in for a surprise to see a woman doing the recitation from the holy book, the key focus in the Gurdwara, and men serving food to people in langar (the communal meal). Both men and women have equal access to initiation and the initiated ones wear the five symbols of the faith. Men and women usually tend to have the same first names, and can only be distinguished by the second name Singh (for men) and Kaur (for women) respectively.

In Sikh history, women have taken a full part in shaping it. Guru Nanak's elder sister Bebe Nanki was the first person who recognised his holiness and became his disciple. Bibi Bhani was the daughter of a Guru, the wife

120

Men are told that they should consider other women as their mothers, daughters and sisters respectively and not as mere sex objects to be exploited.

Men and women should be faithful in marriage and love and respect each other.

(Sikh Code of Conduct)

of a Guru and the mother of a Guru (third, fourth and fifth Gurus). Her contribution to the development of the faith is immense. There are many other women who provided leadership and support to enable the faith to develop, during the period of the Gurus and in later centuries. The Gurus encouraged women to participate in congregational worship, in running the langar and in managing congregational districts. The third Guru, Bibi Bhani's father, ordered his disciples to stop the killing of baby girls, the practise of Sati (the forced burning of widows on the funeral pyre of their dead husbands), and encouraged education for girls, unveiling of their faces, simple weddings without dowries and widow remarriage. These reforms had a tremendous impact on the Sikh community as a whole and on women in particular.

However there is still an imbalance between the preaching of equality and practice. This gap is taking long to bridge. The Sikhs would ideally like to believe that there is equality of men and women in faith. However there are cultural and economic inequalities which affect women and children. Oppression, poverty, lack of education and inequality in career opportunities must be addressed for women to become equal partners in practice. There is also the additional burden of dowry which is contrary to Sikh faith. Medical technology is being used to deny females the chance to be born. Only a concerted effort by political and religious leadership could help remove inequality and create an equitable society.

The Sikh faith is a family faith and it is necessary to lead a family life. Marriage is an important social and religious institution. It is a way of spiritual growth of the two individuals and not only a social and economic device to raise the young. Relationships should be based on love, trust and mutual respect.

Sexual discrimination and exploitation are against the Sikh faith but the patriarchal system in which the community is rooted does not make it possible to eradicate them. We should continue to work together on removing it.

At a wider level, individual families make up communities and need to work towards trust, acceptance and support of each other in this context.

Ideas for exploration.

The Sikhs say that men and women are equal in faith. Could you give any example to illustrate it?

How have social reforms helped women in Sikhism?

A ZOROASTRIAN VIEW OF COMMITMENT TO A CULTURE OF EQUAL RIGHTS AND PARTNERSHIP BETWEEN MEN AND WOMEN

Listen with your ears to the highest truth, consider it with illumined minds carefully and decide each man and woman personally between the two paths, good and evil.

Zarathusthra's message.

GY 30,2

They regard the false ones as great persons, because of their dignity and worldly grandeur, O Lord of Wisdom. They hold back the respectable men and women from attaining their wishes and enjoying God's gifts. They distract the minds of righteous and truthful people and destroy their lives.

GY 32,11

A Now-Ruz HaftShin table. The seven items represent the bounty of the Creator.

Zoroastrians are raised in family homes where boys and girls are equally valued and equally treated. They do not have a tradition of segregation nor of the desirability of one sex over the other. Even the very ancient teachings, the **Gathas,** show an equality of attitude by addressing both men and women which contrasts with most scriptures where normally pronouns suggest that the intended audience is assumed to be male.

In attitudes towards marriage, girls and women are free to decide for themselves whether or not to marry, even in previous times where parents would often take the initial steps in seeking suitable partners. Zoroastrians are not allowed to have more than one wife and divorce was traditionally disapproved of although it did occasionally take place. Marriage is considered a new phase in life where partnership and cooperation is required to make a successful setting for the raising of children. It is understood that a partnership can only be successful if both sides are satisfied with their deal and marriage has to begin and continue on an equal footing.

Women have equal inheritance rights, and are expected to be able to make responsible decisions involving finance, education and politics. Indeed in the past we have had female rulers, and female priests, and in the

When you come within our Brotherhood, and as long as love and faithfulness exist in the hearts of you two young people (wife and husband), whether you strive for this life or the next, you shall reap the best rewards. However, should you leave this Brotherhood and be deluded by the spirit of untruth, then grief and woe shall be your final words.

GY 53, 3 & 7

These words I speak to you maidens, and newly wed husbands, and hope you will bear them in your minds carefully. Understand them deep within your souls and live always full of love with pure mind. Try to surpass each other in truth and righteousness. Thus each one of you shall, indeed, reap the reward of joy and happiness.

Hear and give heed to these truths, O, Men and Women. Strive to avoid the lures of this material life and stop the progress of untruth and deceit.

GY 53, 5–6

more recent past, women were often left as heads of households when their menfolk were away on distant journeys. They then had to make critical decisions concerning the use of land and water, their children's education and the financial resources available to the household.

In terms of social interaction, Zoroastrians have always celebrated and mourned together as is natural in a community where men and women are considered to have complementary roles to play and where each supports the other. It is sometimes said that since no humans can exist without both sexes, their roles are different but of equal importance. Zoroastrian girls are expected to maintain a degree of modesty, but dancing and singing, playing and drinking together does not pose any social difficulty and this appears to have always been the case as our scriptures confirm.

The issue of equal rights is a dimension of tolerance and respect for life and the Zoroastrian position on this question is clear. This is perhaps all the more relevant as the Zoroastrians of Iran are experiencing a loss of human rights since the political climate of late twentieth century Iran is not tolerant nor conducive towards equality for those who do not share the political/theological outlook of the present regime. Zoroastrians have had long experience of not being allowed to enjoy equal rights: right up till the early twentieth century they were discriminated against and not allowed some of the basic rights like riding a donkey, wearing glasses or building a two floor house etc. There are still people alive who can remember being stoned for being Zoroastrian.

Questions:

Do you think men or women get the best deal in society today?

Are there situations where women need more protection or special laws?

The Transformation of Life

A BAHA'I VIEW OF THE TRANSFORMATION OF LIFE

True religion is the source of love and agreement amongst men, the cause of the development of praiseworthy qualities; but the people are holding to the counterfeit and imitation, negligent of the reality which unifies; so they are bereft and deprived of the radiance of religion.

'Abdu'l-Baha, *Baha'i World Faith* 238

The only difference between members of the human family is that of degree. Some are like children who are ignorant, and must be educated until they arrive at maturity. Some are like the sick and must be treated with tenderness and care. None are bad or evil!

'Abdu'l-Baha, *Paris Talks* 138–9

Unquestionably there must be agreement between true religion and science. If a question be found contrary to reason, faith and belief in it are impossible and there is no outcome but wavering and vacilation.

'Abdu'l-Baha, *Baha'i World Faith* 240

As the primary focus of the Baha'i Faith is the coming together of all people, its Writings deal fully with principles and plans for the achievement of world unity and peace.

The first principle is that of the **search for truth** which must be undertaken by every person in order that they grasp the essential knowledge of the existence of truth in all religions. All the religions which have a divine basis have been revealed by the one God so it is not acceptable to cling solely to one form and deny the others.

The second principle states **humankind is one**. As God is Creator of all and the Creator regards all equally, the unity of the world's citizens is ensured – it is a divinely ordained equality which cannot be removed or denied by humans. This makes all people members of one human family; a man-made division violates the principle of unity.

In this physical world, the law of attraction is what holds the elements of each object together, when that power is withdrawn the elements separate and the form ceases to exist. It is the same with the body of humanity – the power which holds the whole together being harmony and unity. Without these forces of attraction, humankind will disintegrate. 'Therefore should every servant of the One God be obedient to the law of love, avoiding all hatred, discord, and strife.'('Abdu'l-Baha, *Paris Talks* 139–140)

The third principle is that **religion must promote** unity and fellowship. It is the divine intention that religion should bring love and agreement, and serve to unite all people. So essential is this principle that should it fail to be a cause of unity, an absence of religion would be preferable.

A further necessary teaching is **the agreement of religion and science**. Superstitions and traditions which have no basis in fact are ignorance. Ignorance gives rise to prejudices which are destructive of human happiness and welfare, so religious belief must be in accord with science.

A fifth essential area of the teachings of the Prophet Baha'u'llah deals with regulations for a **world economy**. These call for a readjustment of social and economic conditions on the grounds of justice for all the world's citizens. Without such readjustment the happiness and prosperity of the world at large is impossible.

I hope that whether you be in the east or the west you will strive with heart and soul in order that day by day the world of humanity may become glorified, more spiritual, more sanctified; and that the splendour of the Sun of Reality may be revealed fully in human hearts as in a mirror. This is worthy of the world of mankind. This is the true evolution and progress of humanity.

'Abdu'l-Baha, *Baha'i World Faith* 262

The recognition of an **equal standard of human rights** is the sixth principle laid down as essential to the progress of the world of humankind. As all people are equal in the sight of God the Creator, any man-made distinctions or preferences are iniquitous and must be abandoned.

The need for **universal education** is also given the status of an essential principle for the establishment of a just world order. All peoples in all countries should receive a good education; there should be international agreement as to a universal curriculum with a global basis of ethics.

Barriers in communication hinder world unity, so the eighth principle is the adoption of a **universal language.** Experts from the world of learning must meet to select a language which will be taught in the schools of all countries so that international communication will be aided by greater understanding and problems caused by misunderstanding avoided.

Equality of man and woman is the ninth principle set down by the Prophet Baha'u'llah. In this age it is essential that the unequal treatment which has characterised the world of humanity in past times is abandoned and women everywhere are given the opportunities to succeed in all fields of life. Without the fulfilment of this divinely ordained principle, the human world will not progress to the elevated station it is destined to achieve.

These basic principles are all essential to establishing full maturity to the world of humankind. They are all necessary in order that human society may be able to attain to a higher level.

Imagine or discuss:

The implications of the establishment of a world economy based on justice for all peoples and nations.

What do you think would be essential to include in a common curriculum for international education?

Make a list of present problems that you can see being avoided by the adoption of a common language to be learned by all nations and races so all could communicate with everyone else.

A BRAHMA KUMARIS VIEW OF THE TRANSFORMATION OF LIFE

Those who conscientiously check and change thoughts, words, or actions which cause disservice to the self or to others stay clean inside and out. The process takes courage, humility, and the recognition that one also comes equipped with the power to **choose.** Each individual sits in the driver's seat and has freedom of choice; to go, stop, turn, merge, yield, signal and so on. We can choose to act based on innermost principles and right values, or we can choose to react based on external negative circumstance. (Living Values)

Some things facilitate learning, and other things destroy it. Arrogance destroys it. 'I know this already' ... have this thought and learning will stop. Also, being tied up in a million things will not help you get into the depth of one thing. You cannot really change until you get into the depth of one thing. When learning stops there is no more change, there is no more progress, and the soul, whose task it is to learn and change, is bereft. (Companion of God)

First of all, do not be afraid of your sins because God will never stop loving you. He knows that love keeps a child growing, so just keep thinking of what He wants you to do and do it. 'Trying to do' will not work; 'trying' does not bring a reward. God's help comes only when there has been effort from the heart; having understood deeply what you want to see changed. Sit with God and ask His forgiveness. He always gives it anyway. Then share, ceaselessly, your experience with others. Then you will begin to feel cleaner, lighter and dear to God (which is) a reminder to others that they can be too. (Companion of God)

There will always be the opportunity to learn for those who desire it. (Companion of God)

Meditation on 'Baba's Rock' at Mt Abu, India, where the headquarters of the Spiritual University are situated.

One of the fundamental principles of the Brahma Kumaris' teachings is, 'When we change, the world changes'. In other words, change on a wider level begins with change within the self.

Life is about change. Just as life presents itself like a drama before us, and every scene is unique and wonderful, so too our responses should be just as creative and new. Change is about learning, accepting, inculcating, checking and then changing.

Every day, students of the Brahma Kumaris World Spiritual University meditate and participate in spiritual study, in order to equip themselves with tools for personal change. When changes begin to happen within the self, it is then expressed in our awareness, thoughts, feelings, vision, attitude, words and actions. In the many educational programmes offered at centres around the world, methods for change are offered through courses such as positive thinking, self-management, stress management and many other life skills.

The Mind

The mind is the most precious resource that we have in effecting a change in consciousness. The power of the mind can reach across space and time, and cross all cultural boundaries. One moment's noble and inspired thought can take a lifetime to express, as seen in the lives of great servers or artists. By contrast, so much time is wasted in generating negative thoughts. An hour, a week, a month, or even years of negative thinking may precede five minutes of expressed anger.

Meditation is considered to be the most effective method for making thoughts truthful, positive and elevated. Meditation is based on the art of understanding how the mind functions. There are three aspects of consciousness.

The mind – the generator of thoughts;

The intellect – the sifter of thoughts, bringing thoughts into action;

The subconscious – the holder of memories and personality traits.

Thoughts are followed by a discernment and decision taking process, after which the memory of each action is impressed upon the sub-conscious. The more often an action is impressed upon the sub-conscious, the stronger is the tendency to repeat that action. In this way habits and personality traits (from compassion or anger to smoking or eating too quickly) build up. When your accumulated habits become your identity, you lose touch with your real self.

Take a few moments to identify a habit that you wish to change. Try to identify the situations that make you respond in that habitual way and observe the pattern of thoughts, discernment, action and reinforcement of that habit over time. Now choose a response, you would prefer, to that same situation and try it out next time. Start to create habits and personality traits of your choice.

The Real Self

The starting point for meditation is to contemplate deeply on the nature of the self. This leads to the experience of the self as a living being of light, a soul, that thinks, feels and acts through the body. The body is the chariot or temple for the soul; without the soul the body is inert, it does not have its own separate consciousness. Such contemplation takes you deeply into the inner resources of the self ... the love, peace, happiness, wisdom and strength that lie within.

Using these inner resources as the basis for outer expression brings about change on all levels – thoughts, feelings, vision, attitude, words and actions. The result is a change in awareness, towards ourselves, others and the world around us. Such awareness provides us with the right consciousness with which to come into relationship with God, from whom we need to draw spiritual power to uphold such change. Such an awareness of my real, spiritual self leaves no room for anger, greed, possessiveness, arrogance or selfishness. We have nothing to lose but everything to give. We are no longer in a state of spiritual emptiness or need, we have a treasure store of spiritual wealth from which to donate. We are able to fill ourselves from the infinite treasure store of God's love, peace, happiness, wisdom and strength, and continue to donate the treasures that we have received in trust. Life lived in this consciousness is a life of natural ethics and right action, that brings happiness to everyone. Virtue becomes the natural law. In a world where all human beings live out virtue in their lives, there is no need for laws, police, courts or prisons. Everyone's life is filled with a natural order and rhythm, such that even nature responds to the positive and elevated consciousness of human beings. Such a world is a world without suffering or peacelessness. Such a world is a world of paradise.

Question:

What does the phrase 'virtue becomes the natural law' really mean for my personal life? Is it possible to live in this way now?

A BUDDHIST VIEW OF THE TRANSFORMATION OF LIFE

In the Chinese Buddhist tradition there is a series of pictures which represents the transformation of life. They are called the ten oxherding pictures. It is the story of a little oxherder who is looking for an ox and how he finds it and tames it.

The first picture is called 'Searching for the ox'. The oxherder is supposed to have an ox to look after so he is looking for one. In the same way we are born into life and for some time we are taken care of by our parents. When we leave home what are we supposed to do? What is the meaning of our life? Is it only about taking care of ourselves and becoming better and richer than other people, regardless of others and the impact we have on the world?

The second picture is called 'Seeing the footprints'. Finally after walking for a long time the oxherder sees some ox footprints. In the same way, we encounter traces of ideas, concepts which ask us to look beyond just ourselves. We hear or read about religions, philosophies, psychologies, various cultural movements which make us think differently or more deeply about ourselves and others.

The third picture is called 'Seeing the ox'. At last the oxherder following the footprints has found and can see the ox. In the same way after a while we find a religion or a philosophy which has a deep meaning for us and for our life in a world shared with others. If we find Buddhism, it encourages us to practice ethics, meditation and wisdom in order to achieve harmony between inner life and the outer world. It is called the 'middle way', a balanced state avoiding self-indulgence or self-sacrifice.

The fourth picture is called 'Catching the ox'. Now that the oxherder has found the ox he has to catch it. The ox is wild, jumping all over the place, it is very hard to hold onto the rope. In the same way, although we have decided to follow Buddhism, it is very hard to cultivate ethics, meditation and wisdom. We find it hard not to be aggressive towards others when we are angry, not to want things which other people have, not to tell lies and not to want intoxicants when we are not feeling well. It is difficult at the beginning to sit still in meditation. We are reluctant to try to reflect on the way we habitually consider things and how that might cause suffering to ourselves and others.

The fifth picture is called 'Herding the ox'. The oxherder is gently tending to the ox and the ox is not

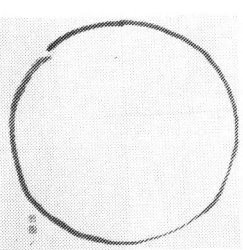

wild anymore. In the same way, when we realise how useful and beneficial Buddhist training can be we start to be more dedicated and by diligently practising ethics, meditation and wisdom, we begin to see changes in ourselves and how we relate to other people.

The sixth picture is called 'Riding the ox back home'. The oxherder and the ox are at ease with each other. They are returning home and the oxherder is playing the flute riding on the back of the ox. After practising for a while we have the same ease and also we become creative. We do not just follow rules. As the qualities of love and compassion become more established, they come more naturally when we think, act or speak.

The seventh picture is called 'Forgetting the ox, the man rests alone'. The ox has disappeared and the oxherder is resting alone at home. At this stage we do not have to practise Buddhism anymore as such. Everything we do intuitively is good but also leisurely. We do not have to force ourselves to do anything special. The way we are is love and compassion. We realise these qualities were there all along, they were only covered by confusion. Through the practice of ethics and meditation, we dissolve the confusion and our true nature which is good can emerge.

The eighth picture is called 'The man and the ox are both forgotten'. There is only a circle. It symbolises peace. After we have practised for some time we become more contented, more aware. We realise and experience that everything is impermanent and changes, nothing can be grasped at, though we can take care of what we have and who we meet. We develop the wisdom of non-grasping which gave us great peace of mind.

The ninth picture is called 'Returning to the original place'. It is a picture of nature, trees and flowers. At that stage, through cultivating wisdom we realise that everything is interdependent. We experience that we are not isolated and separate from the world. We are totally of the world and intrinsically dependent on it. For example we breathe the same air with animals, trees, and the people.

The last picture is called 'Appearing in the market place to teach and transform'. Living life from love and compassion, we have empathy with the suffering of others. Realising interdependence, we feel compelled to help. Developing wisdom and non-grasping, we find appropriate ways truly to benefit the world.

'Truly, truly, unless one is born anew, he cannot see the kingdom of God.' Nicodemus said to Jesus, 'How can a man be born when he is old? Can he enter a second time into his mother's womb and be born? Jesus answered, 'Truly, truly, I say to you, unless one is born of water and the Spirit, he cannot enter the kingdom of God.
John 3: 3-6

Do you not know that all of us who have been baptised into Christ Jesus were baptised into his death? We were buried therefore with him by baptism into death, so that as Christ was raised from the dead by the glory of the Father, we too might walk in newness of life.
Romans 6: 3-4

Do not be conformed to this world but be transformed by the renewal of your mind, that you may prove what is the will of God, what is good and acceptable and perfect.
Romans 12: 2

Therefore if any one is in Christ, he is a new creation: the old has passed away, behold, the new has come.
2 Corinthians 5:17

Love releases the power to love. This is the essence of the Christian way of life. 'In this is love, not that we loved God but that he loved us and sent his Son to be the expiation of our sins.' (1 John 4:10) Another way of putting it is that God offers us an ever fresh and new beginning no matter what we have done, who we have slept with, or who we have robbed or harmed. Christian discipleship then is personal response to the love and forgiveness of God as seen in the life and ministry of Jesus. It is by grace that we can be disciples.

Awareness of this love and the power to change comes in many different ways. A starving young German refugee at the end of World War II is fed by two elderly sisters in the village of Springe near Hannover. Surprised by their kindness he is caught by the spirit they carry and finds himself drawn into Christian fellowship. Later he becomes the pastor of the same congregation.

An African student studying plant breeding at the University of Wales, one evening finds someone sharing their testimony of Christ in the common room and is struck deeply by what he heard.

A teenage girl whose mother has died of cancer and who has then been kicked out by her stepfather, finds herself vulnerably on her own. After being raped, she finds support and a home through a friend's circle of Christian contacts and discovers faith among them.

There are many more stories to be told of encounters in which people experience the kindness of God through circles of Christians and find a joy which surprises them. These stories are very important and in some ways are a continuing of the biblical tradition finding echoes of stories like the parable of the prodigal son (Luke 15:11-32); Peter's denial and forgiveness (Luke 22:54-62, 24:34); the woman caught in adultery (John 8:1-11); Paul's conversion on the road to Damascus (Acts 9:1-20); the Ethiopian Eunuch (Acts 8:26-39) and so on.

Acts of unexpected kindness are transforming moments. So too are moments of repentance when an individual sees the truth about themselves and then to their surprise finds forgiveness and a fresh new start. If the full life is being fully in relationship with others and God, then sin is alienated, broken relationships. Jesus when questioned about the company he kept – tax collectors and sinners – replied

Those who are well have no need of a physician, but those who are sick. Go and learn what this means, 'I desire mercy, and not sacrifice.' For I came not to call the righteous, but sinners. (Matthew 9:12-13):

Sacraments

There are rituals, called sacraments by some Christians and ordinances by others, which catch in dramatic form transforming events in the life of Jesus and connect them with our own story.

Baptism

Baptism is one of these and perhaps finds its clearest and most faithful expression when a young person or adult chooses freely and with full knowledge of the commitment they are making is baptised, particularly by full immersion – symbolising burial and resurrection with Christ. This means everything has to change including one's use of money and property. Confirmation points the individual to the help and continuing transforming support of the Holy Spirit.

Baptism in Southern India. *S.Thangavel,* © USPG.

Communion

Communion, the Lord's Supper, the Eucharist or Mass are all different names for the way different Christians remember the last supper of Jesus, eaten just before his arrest and trial.

Confession

Confession either formally through the confessional in Catholicism or informally with a Christian friend or friends is important for continuing in the Christian way. We are all prodigal children. To speak out one's sins and find loving support rather than condemnation enables them to be left behind.

Marriage

Marriage has already been discussed – but this is another powerful Christian ritual that marks the transformation from being single to being a couple committed to each other for life and joint Christian discipleship.

Ordination

To be set apart through ordination is another transforming experience for particular service that recollects the calling of Jesus' first disciples.

The Laying on of Hands

The laying on of hands for the sick brings healing as well as reassurance. In modern Catholic expression, this sacrament is a sacrament of healing as well as bringing solace to the very ill and dying.

Prayer, meditation, silence, scripture study, worship and fellowship of work and play all help keep the individual Christian connected with others and the transforming grace of God.

Finally, Christianity at its truest, is not just about personal transformation, but also about social and institutional change until everything comes under the Lordship of Christ and the Kingdom of God rules completely. Jesus talked about new wine in new wineskins.

Ideas for exploration:

1. How do Christian sacraments symbolise transformation?

2. 'To be a Christian it is not enough to have Christian parents; one has to also have a personal conversion experience.' Discuss.

3. How are prayer and Bible study important for transformation?

A HINDU VIEW OF THE TRANSFORMATION OF LIFE

For Hindus an awareness for every individual of being interlinked with everything else in the cosmic web is clearly perceived as a matter of consciousness rather than belief or acceptance. For, according to Hindu concepts, this world wide web exists whether we like it or not, and whether we accept it or not. In principle, then, this is the same as other religions, where you either accept the existence of a certain God, or you do not. It is typical of Hinduism, not to deny the existence of all kinds of gods and other superhuman beings, but to incorporate them all into the Hindu worldview.

Hindus, young and old, are made aware of this not so much explicitly – because this universal interlinkedness seems to be taken for granted – but focus instead on individual links with certain deities. Thus, Hinduism today appears to be a more theistic religion, like others. However, this theistic linking does not in fact function in isolation from the world wide web of Hindu Order. It is simply a visible part of it.

Young Hindus today find it often difficult to learn about 'their' tradition because it is so diffuse and confusing. It seems tempting for them to follow the argument that there are good universal principles which should inspire everyone. The trouble is that this new universal religion of goodness and ethical awareness seems to be culture-neutral and, more critically, that it then allocates to Hinduism and Hindu culture only a catalogue of abuses and quaint ideas which do not fit into the global framework of good ethics. Exactly the same has happened in the legal field, where international human rights law claims to be the effective guarantor of human rights while national systems, especially in Asia and Africa, are portrayed as the perpetual violators of basic norms.

It is only when they discover ancient Hindu cultural texts which talk, a thousand years and more ago, about the same values which we debate today as modern and progressive, that they realise that attempts to construct a global moral order are not really new territory. It depends very much on individual reaction what kind of transformation this realisation would bring about. Unfortunately, many Hindus at that stage simply fall back to arguing that Hinduism has always been a universal system and that we have heard everything well before our time. This may be so, but does not advance the present discussion because there is a danger that it ends up in cultural politics.

The realisation that it is important to be good for the sake of others, not for one's own benefit alone, appears to be impeded by confusions over what it means to be good. There are many distractions from simple realisation, and there is also room for disagreement over what is actually good and what is bad, so here is another conundrum. It may help the discussion if we conclude here with the suggestion that an assessment of the morality of an action should not only include a consideration of the immediate present, but also of future consequences.

Questions:

Do you think there is anything very new about attempts to construct a global moral order?

Does the 'new universal religion of goodness' allow for cultural variety?

A JEWISH VIEW OF THE TRANSFORMATION OF LIFE

Judaism believes that human beings were created to be God's partners in the work of bringing the world to perfection – our task as human beings is therefore to do everything we can to ensure that the world is a better place; that ability is what it means to say that we are created in the image of God. If we work enough at it, then we may bring this world to the state of perfection which is its final destiny.

A Better World

Judaism believes that the way to work towards a better world is to keep the various commandments given in the Bible and explained and expanded in later Jewish literature. Judaism recommends detailed specific ethical actions rather than grandiose generalised schemes for perfection. Some prayer-books preface the prayers said before performing the commandments with the words 'I am ready and prepared to fulfil this commandment in order to return God's presence into the world.' The prophetical books insist on the importance of correctly prioritising the various commandments, preferring feeding the hungry and keeping the Sabbath as a day of delight to fasting and offering sacrifices.

> *Is such the fast that I choose, a day to humble oneself? Is it to bow down the head like a bulrush, and to lie in sackcloth and ashes? Will you call this a fast, a day acceptable to the Eternal. Is not this the fast that I choose: to loose the bonds of injustice, to undo the thongs of the yoke, to let the oppressed go free, and to break every yoke? Is it not to share your bread with the hungry, and bring the homeless poor into your house; when you see the naked, to cover them, and not to hide yourself from your own kin? Then your light shall break forth like the dawn, and your healing shall spring up quickly; your vindicator shall go before you, the glory of the Eternal shall be your rear guard. Then you shall call, and the Eternal will answer; you shall cry for help, and God will say, Here I am. If you remove the yoke from among you, the pointing of the finger, the speaking of evil, ... the Eternal will guide you continually, and satisfy your needs in parched places, and make your bones strong; and you shall be like a watered garden, like a spring of water, whose waters never fail. ... If you refrain from trampling the Sabbath, from pursuing your own interests on my holy day; if you call the Sabbath a delight and the holy day of the Eternal honourable; if you honour it, not going your own ways, serving your own interests, or pursuing your own affairs; then you shall take delight in the Eternal ... for the mouth of the Eternal has spoken. (Isaiah 58: 5-14)*

What is religious life? There was an ancient debate: can someone who studies God's teachings intensively but does nothing practical to further the good of the community at large be counted righteous? It was agreed that the community will be made up of four different types, those who practice righteousness and those who prefer to study, those who neither study nor improve society and those who can easily encompass both. It was also felt that the very process of studying God's teachings would inevitably wake up the student to the importance of ethical issues.

In the *Amidah*, the main prayer of Judaism, said three times daily, we ask God to heal the sick, to forgive our sins, to reward the righteous and bring into being the perfect future age of justice and righteousness. Rabbi Lionel Blue says that asking God to do these things reminds us to play our part in doing them.

Transformation of Spirit

Nachman of Bratslav, an eighteenth century mystic and teacher wrote this prayer for peace in which he hoped for a transformation of his spirit.

May the will come from You to annul wars and the shedding of blood from the universe. Nor again shall one people raise the sword against another and they shall learn war no more. But let all the residents of earth recognise and know the innermost truth: that we are not come into this world for quarrel and division, nor for hate and jealousy, contrariness and bloodshed; but we are come into this world to recognise and know, You may you be blessed forever. And let Your glory fill all our wits and minds, knowledge and hearts; and may I be a chariot for the presence of Your divinity. May I not again depart from holiness as much as a hairsbreadth. May I not think one extraneous thought. But may I ever cling to You and to Your sacred teaching until I be worthy to introduce others into the knowledge of the truth of Your divinity. To announce to the children of men Your power, and the honour of the glory of Your kingdom.

Repentance

What to me is the multitude of your sacrifices? Says the Eternal; I have had enough of burnt offerings of rams and the fat of fed beasts; I do not delight in the blood of bulls, or of lambs, or of goats …. Your new moons and your appointed festivals my soul hates; they have become a burden to me, I am weary of bearing them. When you stretch out your hands, I will hide my eyes from you; even though you make many prayers, I will not listen; your hands are full of blood. Wash yourselves; make yourselves clean; remove the evil of your doings from before my eyes; cease to do evil, learn to do good; seek justice, rescue the oppressed, defend the orphan, plead for the widow. Come now, let us argue it out, says the Eternal: though your sins are like scarlet, they shall be like snow; though they are red like crimson, they shall become like wool.

(Isaiah 1: 11–18)

The word for repentance in Judaism is *teshuvah*, returning – when we repent for what we have done wrong, we return to our own best possible selves and to our own innate goodness. The importance of a sense of our own good is seen in another statement of Nachman of Bratslav: 'Before the prayers, remember any good qualities you have, or any good deeds which you have performed. This will put life into you and enable you to pray from the heart.'

There is a famous inscription found on the walls of a cellar where Jews hid from the Nazis which says 'I believe in the sun even when it is not shining. I believe in love even when feeling it not. I believe in God even when He is silent.' If our faith in God and in the power of human love is strong enough, then we can continue to base our lives and our actions on that belief, however terrible the circumstances around us and however hard conditions make it to continue to hold to a positive faith.

Question

Who would you consider a righteous person?

BELIEVERS! Remember God in frequent recollection. Celebrate His praise at dawn and in the evening. It is He who sends down blessing upon you, as do His angels, to bring you forth from the shadows into the light. He is merciful to those who believe. On the day when they meet Him a greeting of 'Peace' will be their welcome. He has made ready for them a gracious reward.

Qur'an 33,4.

Righteousness does not consist in the mere act of facing the *qiblah* of the east or of the west. They have the true righteousness who believe in God and the last Day, in the angels and in the Scripture and the prophets, who spend their substance – prize it lovingly as they may – on their own kinsfolk, and orphans, the impoverished, the wayfarer and those who beg, and on the ransoming of slaves. Theirs is true righteousness who perform the prayer-rite and pay the Zakāt, who fulfill their word when they have given a promise, who endure patiently under distress and hardship and, in time of danger. These are the ones whose faith is genuine: these are the truly God-fearing people.

Qur'an 2,177

When you see one burning with the fire of poverty, broken by his exceeding destitution, draw near to him, for there is no veil between Me and him. Prize as a spoil the intercession of the poor, for they are with Me and I with them.

Al-Ghawthiyya ,'Abd al-Qādir al-Jilāni.

Prayer is one of the Five Pillars of Islam. We must pray five times a day the obligatory prayers. This keeps us aware of God and enables us to refresh our innermost being. The regularity and simplicity of the obligatory prayers gives one respite from the daily grind and helps maintain a healthy perspective. Acts of worship also include the practical such as planting a field, sharing one's knowledge or helping a neighbour.

Islam does not separate the world into religious and secular. It is whole and everything we do is guided by religious principles. The various topics of the Global Ethic discussed above are not mutually exclusive but are intimately intertwined.

> 'For Muslims, anything they do where they do not forget Allah, and where they intend good, is an act of worship – whether it is helping your neighbour or whether it is operating a machine that you work on or driving a car – it is an act of worship if it is done with the right intention. Muslims believe that intentions are the key to success. People cannot always be judged by the outcome of their work. What is important is that they do whatever they do with good intention. So as a way of life, Muslims feel that they have a right to enter into discussion of issues which are not *per se* religious. From an Islamic point of view, they feel that they are qualified to talk about economics, about education, about home affairs, about defence matters, about politics, about social affairs, about things that concern people as they live together. What we endeavour to achieve is a harmonious society where people have the right to abide by their principles, by their set of values.'

John Bowker, *Voices of Islam*, p.32.

Recollectedness of heart is the spirit of the set prayers. The very least that will keep that spirit just gaspingly alive is that the heart shall be present at the moment of *takbir*. Less than that is fatal. Accordingly as there is increase in that recollectedness of heart, the quickening spirit spreads through more parts of the worship. How many living beings are yet without movement, all but dead! Just so the prayer-performance of one who is inattentive beyond the *takbir* is like one alive but lacking movement. *Ihyā'*, 4.3.

16

A SIKH VIEW OF THE TRANSFORMATION OF LIFE

Humans, trees, holy places
Coasts, clouds, fields
Islands, continents, universes
spheres and solar systems
Life forms- egg-born, womb-born,
earth-born, sweat-born
Only God knows their existence,
In oceans, mountains, everywhere
Nanak says, God created them
And God takes care of them

Guru Nanak: Asa di var

There is only one race, the human
race

Guru Gobind Singh

All are free to enter the Gurdwara
without any consideration of caste
or creed. No intoxicant or any
obnoxious thing like tobacco is
allowed to be taken in.

Sikh Code of Conduct

There is a place called City-of-no-
sorrows
There is no grieving, no one suffers
there.
There are no tax-collectors, no one
levies tribute.
There is no worrying, or sin or fear
or death.
My friends, I have found myself a
great place
Where everything is good and
everyone is happy.
Where the Sovereignty of the Lord
is forever
There all are equal, none second or
third.
It is a populous and famous city
The citizens are prosperous
They move as freely as they please
No state official stops them
Says Ravidas, the emancipated
cobbler
My fellow citizen is my friend.

GGS-345

The Sikhs believe that all life is God given, whether human, animal or plant. God is the source of birth, life and death of all beings. The passage in column one gives us a flavour of God, creating and transforming life.

Having brought the world into being, God sustains, nourishes and protects it. A balance between all elements of nature is necessary for the continuation of the universe. Any disruption to the balance brings disaster and distress to the living. We, humans, have responsibility to ensure that balance is maintained. We are all interdependent on each other and it is necessary to remind ourselves of this.

Sikhs are taught by the Gurus to consider that everybody comes from God. If we honour our Gurus and model our lives on their teachings, then we should treat people fairly and equitably. The distinctions of race, colour, gender, caste, religion and region should not stop people expecting to be treated with dignity and respect.

The Sikh Code of Conduct, points not only to values and expectations of good behaviour within the faith, but also with people outside the Sikh community. The Guru's place is open to everyone.

It is important that while making seating arrangements for the congregation in the Gurdwara, no invidious distinction must be made between person and person, a Sikh and a non-Sikh, high caste or low caste. No extra respect is to be paid to an individual, by providing him with a superior seat, a cushion, a chair, or a cot.

Karah Prasad, the sacred pudding should be served, without any distinction of caste or creed.

Non-Sikhs are also allowed to help freely in the maintenance of the kitchen.

Through these practices in their places of worship, the Gurus wanted to establish a system of equity and equality for all.

The Sikh service ends with this prayer.

'Nanak says, O God, through your grace, may there be goodness for all.' Here is the vision for all people. We could all be transformed if the vision in the hymn becomes a reality for all of us on this planet.

Ideas for exploration

1. What in your view is different to today's world in the ideas given in the hymn 'City of no Sorrows'

2. Do you think that various religions can open their places of worship to others?

A ZOROASTRIAN VIEW OF THE TRANSFORMATION OF LIFE

Where are Thy faithful devotees, O Mazda, who being aware of Thy worthy teachings, through Vohuman, will not leave Thee when faced with trouble and distress, but will use those teachings with intellect and will try to spread Thy message. No other individual, except Thee, do I recognize, O my Lord. Therefore, I wish Thee alone to be my shelter and helper through Asha.

GY 34,7

The wise man who propagates the true religion and makes the people aware of my holy message, which leads them to perfection and immortality, shall enjoy the highest bliss. He shall, no doubt, enjoy Ahuras power too, which increases through pure mind.

GY 31,6

One who always thinks of his own safety and profit, how can he love the joy-bringing Mother Earth? The righteous man that follows Asha's Law shall dwell in regions radiant with Thy Sun, the abode where wise ones dwell.

GY 50,2

The Zoroastrian community is a minute one because of the fortunes of history, and its recent experiences mirror older ones in that they have been forced to migrate and are to be found almost all over the world. 1000 years ago they went to India; today they are on every continent. This dispersal or *diaspora* means that Zoroastrians are very conscious of not having the advantage of a neighbourhood of fellow-believers to spread the teachings and ideas through community example in addition to that set by the family.

It should be pointed out that many Parsees who do not know the **Gathas** are ignorant of the several references to spreading the message. They believe that it is a fundamental tenet of the faith that willing converts should *not* be welcome. The texts clearly belie their mistaken belief.

Furthermore the developments of the late twentieth century in countries following a Western model appear to have had the effect of distracting children towards a consumer rather than a spiritual world outlook. Alongside this we have seen the increasing liberalism within families which partly explains the loosening of parental authority and the loss of inculcation of family traditions and values. This applies equally to Zoroastrian children, who possibly through a desire to integrate into their host communities quickly, tend soon to forget their mother tongue and the associated cultural and religious practices.

However, since the essence of Zoroastrian teachings are ethical precepts, concerned with creating a harmonious society in this life, it matters little whether they are labelled Zoroastrian or merely humanist. The important thing to a true Zoroastrian is not necessarily to see the world acknowledging the source of the inspiration, but to see the inspiration spreading to encompass the world. If all people were to act in keeping with the maxim of good thoughts, words and deeds, and if those deeds incorporated honesty and truthfulness, charity, ecological stewardship and responsibility, adequate agriculture and sufficient clean water, cleanliness and hygiene, and an ability to contemplate, praise and preserve the beauty and balance of nature, then the Zoroastrian's ideal would have been achieved.

O, the Guardian of freedom and worthy of praise, O Lord of Life and Wisdom, I shall gain entrance to Thy Abode with praise and shall join Thee through Truth and Pure Thought. Do guide me, O my Lord, and help me in my tasks.

GY 50,7

Khashathra, the strength divine, is the most precious gift which drops like gentle rain upon our earth, urging the inner selves of those who dedicate their lives through Asha for the service of mankind. O Mazda, paradise is gained by good deeds. Therefore, I shall always try to fulfil good actions.

GY 51,1

Zoroastrian ethics are not excessively concerned with the afterlife although there is a strong eschatological tradition in the religion which has influenced Judaism and Christianity. It is not overly obsessed with what happens next, but with achieving a happy and balanced existence now. Nevertheless, it is important to a Zoroastrian to be able to approach death with a clear conscience and with a light load because according to our traditions, at death we all have to pass across a bridge of judgement. There, if our good deeds throughout our lives outweigh our bad deeds, then we will pass into the realm of light in the company of our guardian angels who look after all aspects of God's creation. However, if our bad deeds are preponderant, then we will plunge into an eternally dark abode. Thus if incentives and beliefs are necessary to keep a person on the right track they can be found in the religious tradition.

However, I and many other 'modern' Zoroastrians believe that the moral principles are the fundamentally important aspects of our religion. If all people come to grasp that there are right and wrong ways to behave and the basic principles of ethical dualism are established throughout society, then the cultural and religious traditions can be treated as interesting historical dimensions of human evolution.

Having stated such a radical position, undoubtedly more conservative voices within our community will refute such an assertion as they proudly guard and preserve the ancient legacy that has passed from the fifteenth century BCE to the twentieth century CE.

Question:

Do you think the moral teaching of a religion is its most important component/message?

SECTION E

A Response from a Non-Religious Viewpoint

ETHICS AND GLOBAL PROBLEMS FROM A NON-RELIGIOUS VIEW-POINT

This contribution is not written from any worldview or religious standpoint. It attempts, instead, to conform to the title of the present volume by testing the Declaration toward a Global Ethic[1], that is offering a critical examination of the ideas and claims in the Declaration. My main purpose in doing this is to try to understand what ethical thinking we need in seeking to solve certain global problems. Throughout the paper, I treat 'ethics' and 'morality' as meaning the same, mindful that in philosophy they often do not.

1. Does Global Ethics have a Moral Basis?

The Declaration Toward a Global Ethic, together with its four principles, including the four irrevocable directives which make up the third principle, attempts to do two things. First, it proposes **a moral basis**, which is said to underpin global ethics. Second, it suggests that there are **concrete standards**, also described as 'four broad, ancient guidelines', which are implied or which arise from this moral basis. The guidelines both provide us with a general statement of the content of global ethics and also themselves provide a basis from which even more specific moral principles for global ethics are derived. Taken all together, this edifice of the basis, the four guidelines and the various specific moral principles are said to provide us with the morality to tackle global problems.

What is this moral basis, and what makes it a moral basis? The authors of the Declaration have tried to identify a common set of core values found in the teachings of the world's religions. This is a risky enterprise because it makes it unclear what one is to say if some religion rejects the proposed set of core values. In the present volume for example, it is clear that the Rastafarians have a general doubt about the justifiability of the moral contents of the Declaration. Do doubts like these somehow undermine the whole enterprise?

Leaving that to one side, what is this claimed commonly agreed basis of morality? A first stab at this is that 'every human being must be treated humanely'. This is closely followed by the remark that every human being 'possesses an inalienable and untouchable dignity'. From this we move to the moral principles that 'humans must be ends, never mere means' and that 'every human is obliged to do good and avoid evil'. Finally, there is said to be a moral principle, one which 'is found and has persisted in many religious and ethical traditions of humankind for thousands of years', and this is 'what you do not wish done to yourself, do not do to others' or in more positive terms 'what you wish done to yourself, do to others'. From this principle (the well-known Golden Rule), the four irrevocable directives are said to arise, these in essence being principles proscribing killing, and demanding a just order, truthfulness and tolerance, and gender equality(p.23 ff).

One way of understanding this set of remarks is to see how they might be connected together. One famous attempt to do this is found in the work of the 18th century German philosopher Kant[2]. Kant was highly critical of any approach to morality which makes good actions dependent or conditional on other things. Thus shopkeepers who give the right change only or mainly to attract custom or preserve their reputation do the right thing but not because it is right. For Kant, for an action to be of moral worth, it had to be done with good intent, out of a goodwill, and not for more calculating reasons.

This, of course, prompts the question of which actions are unconditionally good. Here, Kant does not give us a list of actions, nor even a list of definitive moral principles. Instead, he provides **a method,** the Categorical Imperative, which authors of the Global Ethic claim is used in the world's religions, and which is said to be the basis for morality. What did Kant's Categorical Imperative propose? Think of some action you are proposing. Then ask what would it be were **everyone** to act like this. If we apply that test and find that the proposed course of action becomes impossible, it cannot be a moral act. This is the test of **universalising** one's action. Kant provides a number of examples to support this point, not all of which have been found convincing. The most plausible one concerns keeping promises. Suppose you have made a promise, knowing that you will not keep it (you borrow some money saying you will return it but never intending to). Suppose every one did this. Then 'promise-keeping' as we understand it would become impossible because no one would trust anyone when they made a promise. So, Kant claims, that shows that promise-breaking cannot be a moral act, cannot be morally obligatory.

What does this show? Kant seems to have shown that any act which becomes impossible when everyone performs that kind of act, cannot be one we have a moral obligation to do. Making false promises cannot be a moral obligation. But does this also show that the opposite of this, keeping the promises one has made, is morally obligatory? Clearly, 'keep the promises one has made' is the sort of act which when everyone does it, is a possible act. There is nothing remotely resembling it being an impossible act. But does this being a possible act show that it is an act we must do? The reasoning here would be that since making a promise, not intending to keep it and not keeping it, must be wrong, so the opposite of this, making a promise, intending to keep it and keeping it, must be both right, and so must be what we are morally obliged to do.

In similar fashion, if we 'translate' Kant's idea into that of the Golden Rule, we might say that if a person, X, makes a promise, X's being obliged to keep it can be shown by asking how X would respond if someone else, Y, made a promise to X and then broke it. The inference here is that X would not like that, and so, since Y too would not like it if X did that to Y, consistency requires that X keep the promises which X makes (and likewise when Y and everyone else make promises).

Kant thought that if we use his method in ethics, we will be able to work out what is morally right and morally wrong. We would have moral knowledge, and we would know what our moral obligations were. Indeed Kant also thought, as the authors of the Global Ethic think, that the Categorical Imperative/Golden Rule method entailed that people must always treat others as ends and not mere means, and it is not difficult to see why he thought this. For, to return to the example of promise-keeping, if X makes a promise to Y, never intending to keep it, then X is using Y for X's own goals and is not treating Y as anything other than a mere means to these goals.

How successful is this as the method of finding out what our moral obligations are? Unfortunately, it seems to allow certain principles as moral principles which are either trivial or morally questionable. Take triviality. Suppose I say that whenever I get some dirt in my eye, I ought to turn to the west. This seems universalisable; 'everyone, whenever you get dirt in your eye, turn to the west'. But that cannot be a **moral** command. More seriously, and using one of Kant's own examples, suppose we are considering whether we have a moral obligation to help those who are in need of help, a question which is clearly of importance when considering whether the rich nations ought to help the poor nations. Consider someone who denies that this is a moral obligation, and who thinks that when people are in difficulties, they should just sort things out for themselves. Now apply Kant's universalising test. This enjoins 'everyone: no one has a moral obligation to help anyone in need of help'. This does not seem to be an impossible or incoherent position, and so is different from the case of making false promises, where everyone's doing this would make 'I promise you to do this' became something which no-one would believe. One can even conceive of there being a possible world in which no-one helps anyone, a world of rugged, self-reliant individuals. In such a world, even when one person actually does need help from others, the Kantian method seems incapable of showing that there is a moral obligation to help. And that appears to go against a deep-rooted moral belief, that we help those who are in need of help, the homeless, the sick, the hungry and so on. Kant's method, and its close cousin, the Golden Rule, seem not to deliver what we take to be a moral obligation in this case.

There are other problems too with this approach to ethics, one in particular being the absolutist nature of at least some of the moral obligations which, according to Kant, arise from the application of the method. Suppose we grant that Kant has shown that promise-keeping is morally obligatory. Then does this mean that there can be no circumstances in which a promise might not be set aside because there is a different and more weighty moral obligation pressing itself upon us? Recall that Kant holds that our moral obligations are unconditional, and that acts done conditionally have no moral worth. This must mean that we cannot be doing a

The philosopher Immanuel Kant in a pencil portrait by hans Veit Schnoor von Carolsfeld (1764–1841) © Kupferstich-Kabinett, Staatliche Kunstsammlungen Dresden.

moral act if we say something like 'keeping our promises is the right thing to do, unless there are circumstances which weigh against this', because that is to think conditionally. But as against Kant, there seem to be no moral obligations which cannot clash with other moral obligations. Indeed, this seems to be a regular part of morality, one which makes it so difficult to decide in particular cases what ought to be done. To be fair to Kant, he does appear to have agreed that some duties, 'imperfect duties' as he called them, are such that we cannot obey their call every time they are relevant, though his reason for saying this seems to have been that it is impossible for us to do all the time what ideally we ought to do. But he also thought that this was not true of all moral duties. Some moral duties are 'perfect' and this seems to mean that they hold whatever the circumstances. Yet even the moral obligations not to make false promises and to keep one's promises clash with other moral obligations, and Kant appears to have to take the implausible line of making these absolute, that is ones which cannot ever be set aside.

Where does that leave us? We might make the move of regarding the methods of the Categorical Imperative and the Golden Rule as useful heuristic devices in working out our moral obligations but no more than that. Perhaps, then, we might turn to Kant's moral insight, clearly echoed in the Declaration, that we should never treat persons as mere means to our ends but as ends in themselves. We might treat this as a fundamental moral principle from which all other moral principles and rules can be derived. Being fundamental, it cannot itself be justified. And maybe in ethics, we have to start somewhere. Why not here? But what does it mean to say that we ought to treat all persons as ends and not mere means to our ends? This seems to invite us to treat persons as beings who have goals, purposes, projects, which they should be undisturbed in pursuing, subject only to the constraints of all being allowed to do this. Provided, then, that X's pursuit of her goals does not prevent Y's pursuit of his goals, X should be allowed to get on with her life. This clearly celebrates the freedoms and the autonomy of the individual. That is where the difficulties start. Some people hold that the exercise of one's freedoms, the shaping of one's life around the notion that one can decide how one is to live one's life oneself, places too much emphasis on freedom as a moral value. Moral obligations, for example, the obligation to help those who need help, should take precedence over individual freedoms and autonomy. The trouble with the Kantian approach, so this objection goes, is that it loads the dice in favour of moral autonomy from the start.

Another difficulty resides in the injunction not to treat others as mere means to one's own ends. This cannot mean that we are not to use other people. I might phone someone up because they have some information which is useful to me. I might employ someone because their knowledge and skills are useful for the production of my firm's products. What does the term 'mere' rule out? We might say that it rules out any treatment of another which disregards that other as a person and treats the other as a mere thing. But it is not at all clear what this does rule out. It is not obvious that it even rules out slavery per se, because one can envisage a slave owner who took good care of her slaves and treated them well. This is not to say, of course, that the practice of slave-ownership is morally good. It might not even rule out torture since the torturer knows full well that what they are doing to their prisoner is calculated to bear results because the other **person** cannot take the pain. The torturer, to get results, has to recognise that the other is a person.

There are other problems with Kant's principle which are worth mentioning, albeit briefly, because they have a bearing on global ethics. Kant's emphasis on the importance of treating persons as ends in themselves, seems to confine our moral obligations to those who can have goals, purposes or projects, this being possible because of their use of their rational capacities. This seems to make those who are not yet persons, or who have ceased to be persons, into those to whom we cannot have direct obligations. It would also appear to make those beings who cannot be persons, animals for example, into beings to whom we have no obligations. Kant himself famously remarked that 'our duties towards animals are merely indirect duties towards humanity'[3]. On that account, we might help Tiddles down from the tree but only because Tiddles' plight upsets her owner. Tiddles herself has no moral claim on us. Again, the problem with this is that, as a foundational moral principle, it rules out certain moral judgements from the start. If we have no moral obligations to animals, we need to know why, rather than just to be told that this is not part of morality itself.

To conclude this section, my argument has been that Kantian-type attempts to ground morality by employing the method of universalising, fail, as will Kantian-type attempts to produce a basic moral principle around the notion of treating people as ends and not as mere means to one's own ends. The Declaration bases global ethics on this sort of moral foundationalism, and so this part of its argument does not succeed. Whether we could find some other method or some other basic supreme, moral principle, stretch beyond the confines of this paper. But we might, to move the argument on, not need these. Why not go to moral principles with a specific moral content? This takes us to the four directives, and to the question of whether these can give moral guidance to us as we struggle with global problems.

2 Global Problems and Global Ethics

The Declaration toward a Global Ethic covers matters of war and peace, tolerance and truthfulness, and gender equality. In the space I have available, I leave these to one side and concentrate on what the Declaration has to say about world hunger and about environmental issues.

The Declaration draws attention to some of the appalling conditions which human beings suffer from and endure in the modern world. Most commentators agree that around twenty per cent of the world's population 'live in absolute poverty: hunger, malnutrition, widespread disease, high infant mortality, squalid living conditions, fear and insecurity' and that whilst these conditions can be found in the developed world, most of the twenty per cent 'live in the poorer countries of the world, the developing countries'[4]. It is worth reminding ourselves that twenty per cent of the world's population is, at a conservative estimate, at lest a thousand million people, something like eighteen times the population of the UK, or three and a half times the population of the USA or of the European Union.

The causes of this massive deprivation, of this antithesis of the conditions in which people can live good, decent lives, are various and complex. Some suffer these conditions, and additionally the fears of insecurity, due to their being caught up in wars. The causes of these wars are themselves various and complicated. Others suffer these conditions not because of wars but due to a further complex of causes. It is too simple just to attribute one sort of cause here, as some are inclined to do, blaming starvation and low living standards solely or mainly on shifts in agricultural practice as third world economies are forced into cash-crops and away from traditional subsistence agriculture. There are other causes too. Crops fail just due to the weather, or are insufficient because populations rise faster than the carrying capacities of their economies. Crops fail because of failures to prevent soil erosion due to commercial deforestation, or because traditional slash and burn practices fail to take account of changing climatic conditions. The causes of the poverty, hunger, high mortality rates and so on, need detailed empirical analysis and investigation rather than sweeping generalisations.

We call these problems 'global', I suppose, not just because they affect significant numbers of the world's population, and not just because they affect these numbers in geographically specific locations such as large parts of Africa, but because the existence of poverty on such a scale and in such areas is seen to be a problem not just for the people living such blighted lives but for those who live relatively (and for some absolutely) prosperous lives in the developed world. Is it a moral option just to stand idly by? But layered across these problems of third world poverty is another set of global problems, 'global' this time because what happens in one part of the earth, and its biosphere, has or threatens severe effects on either other specific areas of the earth and biosphere, or on all part of the earth and its biosphere. Chopping down the rain forests, pumping greenhouse gases into the atmosphere, the effects of releasing certain chemicals on the ozone layer, mean that climates and atmospheres are changing far away from the places where these events and states of affairs are located.

World Population Growth, Major Areas

Region	1750	1800	1850	1900	1950	1994	2000	2050
Population Size (Millions)								
Africa	106	107	111	133	224	708	833	2145
Asia	502	635	809	947	1403	3403	3744	5761
Europe	163	203	276	408	549	726	730	678
Latin America and the Caribbean	16	24	38	74	166	474	524	839
Northern America	2	7	26	82	166	290	306	839
Oceania	2	2	6	13	28	31	46	389
Total	**791**	**978**	**1262**	**1650**	**2520**	**5630**	**6168**	**9857**

Source UN Population Division

To make matters even more complex, these problems of world poverty and environmental threat, interact. Some third world countries have policies of rapid industrialisation and urbanisation to deal with their poverty problems, but these just add to global environmental problems and ironically add yet further to the poverty they were meant to alleviate.

We certainly need to understand the many and varied causes of poverty, and the complexities of change in the natural environment. We need to know also, as far as we can, what the effects may be if we adopt this policy or that policy in our attempts to solve these difficulties. But, complicated though these empirical inquiries are, it is tempting to think that the question of what our moral goals ought to be, is obvious and uncontroversial. Is it not obvious that our goal must be to make life decently tolerable for all the people of the earth so that they are not permanently malnourished, or do not die of hunger, or of easily curable disease? Is not it obvious too that whatever economic development best serves these ends is shaped so that the global-wide threats to our biospheric environment are removed?

Against this suggestion, I want to maintain that the empirical questions are not the only difficult questions here. There are a number of alternative moral goals, and we need to do some hard moral thinking before we reach conclusions about what we ought to do.

What position does the Declaration take on these problems? It provides us with a seemingly simple moral principle, calling on all religious people, and moral people generally, to give an 'irrevocable commitment' to solidarity and a just economic order. What does this mean? On closer examination, the Declaration is ambivalent, giving two, mutually exclusive, interpretations of this core global value.

The first is found in these remarks (p.28):

'If the plight of the poorest billions of humans on this planet is to be improved, the world economy must be structured more justly. The participation of all states and the authority of international organisations are needed to build just economic institutions'.

The world economy today is the economy of the free market. Even the People's Republic of China is adopting the practices and institutions of free-market capitalism. The world economy is an economy of free trade, based on the removal of barriers to trade enshrined in the former GATT treaty. It is an economy where goods produced all over the world by individuals and by privately owned and managed corporations are traded all over the world. It is an economy where interest rate movements, or even just their possible movements can trigger changes in share prices all over the world. It is an economy where key corporations themselves are multinational. It is an economy which allows huge diversity in the levels of property ownership and wealth. It is an economy of demand, supply and price.

It is also an economy where some control is exercised over economic activity. Nations and other groups come together to fix prices and control supply. It is also an economy with institutions which provide aid for economic growth.

So we can see the Declaration as proposing that this world-wide economic system is the one to work with, but that it should be shaped so that the wealth it produces is distributed 'more justly', though it does not say what that phrase means. 'Justice' is a notoriously difficult concept to understand, and we are owed some view of what counts as just and unjust acts and why.

There is, however, a second position running alongside this. Here people are urged to be less materialistic and less consumption-driven, and less accepting of the profit-driven free market. The dominance of humanity over nature must not be encouraged. Instead we must cultivate living in 'harmony with nature'(p.26). Distinctions are drawn between 'necessary and limitless consumption', between 'beneficial and non-beneficial uses of property', between 'justified and unjustified uses of natural resources', between 'a profit-only and a socially beneficial and ecologically oriented market economy' (p.28).

This position traces the ills of environmental degradation to the growth in production of goods and services which is the result of the world-wide free-market economy. More radical than the first approach, it proposes that these ills will only be cured if there is fundamental alteration in people's demands, away from cars, white goods, and the whole paraphernalia of the modern economy and towards a simpler, more modest way of life, exemplified perhaps in the kind of life reputed to be lived by the Old Order Amish in the USA

Are these the only alternatives to dealing with the problems of poverty and environmental degradation? On the poverty problem, one contemporary writer presents the following possibilities, only some of which are echoed in the Declaration's two approaches[5]:

a) the problems of third world hunger etc. are best dealt with by **not** offering any assistance from the developed world. The latter has no moral obligation to assist the third world because to provide assistance is to encourage the growth of populations which will outstrip the capacities of the economies of the third world to sustain. Assistance, in other words, will just make matters worse[6]:

b) assistance to the third world is a moral obligation for the developed world, but this should only take the negative form of preventing any development which would threaten the existing cultures and ways of life of the third world:

c) assistance to the third world is an obligation for the developed world but that this is inherently paternalistic and so should be confined to meeting basic needs, leaving the countries and cultures of the third world to find their own ways forward after basic needs have been met:

d) assistance to the third world is an obligation for the developed world and this should take the form of encouraging the most efficient uses of resources, and this is best done (and can be shown to be so) only within a predominantly market economy. The obligations, therefore, amount to removing major impediments to free-market development in third world countries such as the redemption of third world debt, easing barriers to trade, and improving the terms of trade:

e) assistance to the third world is a moral obligation for the developed world and should take the form of a massive redistribution of resources from the latter to the former, this being the most justified form of a just world economic order[7].

When we turn to environmental problems, another contemporary writer, J.R.Elliot, has proposed the following main alternatives[8]:

a) human interests are the only interests which are of significant worth. This is consistent with taking a long-term view of human interests. On the long-term view, we ought to treat the environment in ways which enable long-term human interests to be sustained. So, for example, one could argue for economic development which rejected the use of non-renewable resources, or which used non-renewable resources sparingly or which used them only if the attempt was being made to move over to renewable resources:

b) humans are not the only beings who have interests. Sentient creatures do too, and their interests ought to be taken into account, though it would not follow that their interests had equal weight with human interests:

c)   the same as b) except that animal interests are accorded equal weight with human interests. This ethic would seem to favour the maximisation of the diversity of animal species:

d)   the class of all living things deserves moral consideration. This 'life-centred' ethic would make us morally obliged to preserve all types of living thing, whether animal or not, though it would allow use of them provided the use did not lead to the destruction or degradation of their species or type:

e)   all things, whether living or not, deserve moral consideration. This would make us protect and preserve deserts, mountains and the seas, not because they provide habitats for creatures and other living things and not because they provide resources for human, but because they have worth in themselves.

If we concentrate on trying to deal just with world poverty, we have a human-centred ethic, with various alternatives which differ in terms of whether or not assistance should be given to the third world, and if so what type and amount of assistance should be given. If we concentrate on trying to combat environmental damage and degradation, our ethical choices range from being just human centred to including increasingly wider types of existence.

We have to do some hard thinking about these alternatives, assessing their advantages and disadvantages.

A lot more work needs to be done on global ethics.

Questions

1.   Can you think of a moral principle which **would** provide the basis for global ethics?

2.   Do you think rich nations should help poorer countries? Why?

3.   Should the concern to protect the environment seek to preserve human life or all life?

REFERENCES

1. Küng, H and Kuschel, K.J., *A Global Ethic.*
2. Kant, E., *Groundwork to the Metaphysic of Morals.*
3. Kant I, *Lectures on Ethics* p 239.
4. Dower, N, 'World Poverty' in *A Companion to Ethics*, Ed. Singer, P
5. *Ibid*
6. Hardin, G. *'Lifeboat Ethics'*
7. Singer, P. *Famine, Affluence and Morality'*
8. Elliot, R.. 'Environmental Ethics', in *A Companion to Ethics*, Ed. Singer P.

SECTION F1

Resources

USEFUL INFORMATION AND ADDRESSES

The Bahá'í Faith began in 1844 with the declaration of a new religion by the *Báb* (1819-1850), who heralded the coming of *Bahá'ulláh* (The Glory of God, 1817-1892). Báhá'is believe in the unity of God, the oneness of humankind, the common foundation of all religions and the establishment of universal peace by a world government. The scriptures consist of the *Writings* of the *Báb, Bahá'u'lláh* and *'Abdu'l-Bahá.* There are about 5 and a half million Bahá'is located in over 200 countries. Bahá'is in Iran suffer much persecution.

The Bahá'i Community of the United Kingdom, 27 Rutland Gate, London SW7 1PD.

Bahá'i National Center of the USA, 536 Sheridan Road, Wilmette, IL 60091 USA.

Bahá'i National Center of Canada, 7200 Leslie St., Thornhill, Ontario L3T 6L8 Canada.

Bahá'i World Centre: P.O. Box 155, 31001, Haifa, Israel.

The Brahma Kumaris World Spiritual University is based on the teachings of Dada Lekh Raj (1877-1969), whose spiritual name was Prajapita Brahma. It is a NGO in general consultative status with the Economic and Social Council of the United Nations and UNICEF. The movement believes that the soul is eternal and that through meditation, *Raja Yoga,* people can experience consciousness of the soul and awareness of its eternal relationship with the Supreme Soul. 'The Million Minutes for Peace' and the 'Global Co-operation for a Better World' projects reached 129 countries. *Living Values: A Guidebook* is a publication resulting from the project 'Sharing Our Values for a Better World'.

The Brahma Kumaris World Spiritual University, Global Co-operation House, 65 Pound Lane, London NW10 2HH.

Global Harmony House, 46 S. Middle Neck Rd., Great Neck, NY 11021 USA.

Brahma Kumaris International Headquarters, P.O. Box 2, Mount Abu, 307501, Rajasthan, India.

Buddhism began historically in the 6th and 5th centuries BCE, with the enlightenment of Sidhartha Gautama, also known as Sakyamuni, who, in the Four Noble Truths taught the way to be free of the 'unsatisfactoriness' (*dukka*) of life by following the Noble Eightfold Path. Buddhists do not see the Ultimate as a personal deity. The Buddha's teachings were gathered over a long period into canonical collections, especially the Tripitaka and the Mahayana Sutras. There are over 300 million Buddhists, most of whom follow either the Theravada or the Mahayana tradition.

The Buddhist Society, 58 Eccleston Square, London SW1V 1PH.

Buddhist Churches of America, 1710 Octavia St., San Francisco, CA 94109 USA.

Soka Gakkai International-USA, 525 Wilshire Boulevard, Santa Monica, CA 90401 USA.

Won Buddhism of America, 143-42 Cherry Ave, Flushing, NY 11355 USA.

World Fellowship of Buddhists, 33 Sukhumvit Road, Bangkok 10110, Thailand.

Christianity is named after Jesus Christ who lived in Palestine early in the 1st century CE. He died on a cross and Christians, who hold that Jesus was both fully human and fully God, believe that three days later he was raised from the dead by God. Jesus' life and teaching are recorded in the Gospels which are part of the New Testament, which makes up the last part of the Christian Bible. There are about 1,955 million Christians, mostly belonging either to Roman Catholic, Orthodox, Protestant, Anglican or Pentecostalist churches.

Council of Churches for Britain and Ireland, Inter-Church House, 35-41 Lower Marsh, London SE1 7RI.

The National Council of Churches of Christ in the USA, 475 Riverside Dr., New York, NY 10115-0050 USA.

Hinduism is the name given to the major, but very varied religious tradition of India, often referred to as *Sanatana Dharma* (Eternal Way of Life). Most Hindus believe in One Supreme Reality, usually known through one of many gods, such as Shiva or Visnu. Hindus hold that the soul is eternal and passes through many lives. The law of *karma* means that all actions have consequences. The most sacred scriptures are the four Vedas, although the *Bhagavad Gita* is the most popular holy book. There are over 800 million Hindus, of whom the majority live in India, although there are now Hindu communities in many parts of the world.

Hindu Council of the UK. c/o 150 Penn Road, Wolverhampton, West Midlands, WV3 0EN.

International Society of Divine Love, 243 Avenue Road, Toronto, Ontario M5R 2J6, Canada.

Self-Realization Fellowship, 3880 San Rafael Avenue, Los Angeles, CA 90065 USA.

Vivekananda Foundation, PO Box 1351, Alameda, CA 94501 USA.

Vishwa Hindu Parishad of America, 43 Valley Road, Needham, MA 02192 USA.

Jains are followers of the *Jinas* or Spiritual Victors or teachers, also known as *Tirthankaras* (Ford-makers), of whom the 24th was Mahavira, who is said to have been born in 599 BCE. Jains emphasise Ahimsa or non-violence, which is to be applied to all living beings. Jains do not believe in a personal or creator God. The Jain scriptures are the *Shutra, Agamas* or *Siddhanta.* There are some 6 million Jains, most of whom live in India.

Institute of Jainology, Unit 18, Silicon Business Centre, 26-28 Wandsworth Road, Greenford, Middlesex, UB6 7JZ.

Jain Academy, 20 St James Close, London NW11 9QX.

Jain Samaj Europe, Jain Centre, 32 Oxford Street, Leicester, LE1 5XU.

Federation of Jain Associations in North America, 11820 Triple Crown Road, Reston, VA 22091 USA.

Islam. Muslims who belong to the religion of Islam enter into peace with God by submission to God. This religion was proclaimed by the Prophet Muhammad in the 6th century CE. The messages that Muhammad received from God are written down in Arabic in the Holy Qur'an. The Five Pillars of Islam are belief in One God and that Muhammad was God's messenger; Ritual prayer five times a day; Almsgiving (*Zakat*); an annual month of fasting (*Ramadan*); and Pilgrimage to Mecca (*Hajj*). There are nearly 1,200 million Muslims divided between Sunnis and Shi'ites. Many live in Arab countries and in Malaysia and Indonesia, but there are large Muslim communities in many countries.

Imams and Mosques Council, 20-22 Creffield Road, London W5 3RP.

The Islamic Cultural Centre, 146 Park Road, London NW8 7RG.

Muslim College, 20-22 Creffield Road, London W5 3RP.

Council of Masajids, 99 Woodview Dr., Old Bridge, NY 08857 USA.

Muslim World League, 1655 N. Fort Myer Dr., #700, Arlington, VA 22209 USA.

The Islamic Society of North America (ISNA), P.O. Box 38, Plainfield, IN 46168 USA.

Judaism centres on faith in One God who rescued the Jewish people from slavery in Egypt through Moses early in the 13th century BCE. Jews believe themselves chosen to be a holy people called into a covenant relationship with God who gave them the *Torah* (Law or Teaching) at Mt Sinai. The Jewish sacred scriptures to be found in the Bible are often known as the *Tenakh*, although Christians call them the Old Testament. From the 2nd century CE, a massive literature, including the Talmud, was developed by the Rabbis. There are about 14 million Jews, divided between Orthodox and Progressive Jews, of whom the majority live either in Israel or North America.

The Board of Deputies of British Jews, Commonwealth House, 1-19 New Oxford Street, London WC1A 1NF.

Central Conference of American Rabbis, 192 Lexington Ave., New York, NY 10016 USA.

Council of Jewish Federations, 1640 Rhode Island Ave. NW, Washington, DC 20002 USA

Rabbinical Council of America, 275 7th Ave., 15th Floor, New York, NY 10001 USA.

Rastafarians are named after *Ras* (Prince) Tafari who in 1930 became Emperor Haile Selassie I of Ethiopia and who is seen as the 225th descendent of King Solomon. Following his physical 'disappearance', the presence of Haile Selassie can still be accessed as *Jah*. The phrase 'I and I' refers to the indwelling of *Jah* in human beings. *Babylon* symbolises the godless system of the Western world which is destined to collapse. Life outside Africa is regarded as exile, but with the hope of an Exodus or return to Ethiopia. Rastafarians emphasise the importance of living in harmony with nature. The Bible is regarded as a divine Word, to be interpreted according to Rastafarian teaching.

The Rastafarian Society, 290-296 Tottenham High Road, London N15 4AJ.

Association of Rastafarian Theologians, 843 West Van Buren, Suite 1760, Chicago, IL 60607 USA.

Sikhism is based on the teachings of the ten Gurus, of whom the first was Guru Nanak Dev (1469-1539), who received revelations from God. Sikhism is strictly monotheistic and emphasises universal love, peace, human equality and respect for all religions. The tenth Guru, Gobind Singh, in 1699 established the Khalsa of initiated Sikhs, in whom he vested temporal authority, whilst putting spiritual authority for the community in the *Guru Granth Sahib*, which are Sikh sacred scriptures. Namdhari Sikhs, a small minority, believe in a continuing succession of living Gurus. There are about 20 million Sikhs, of whom eighty per cent live in the Punjab.

Network of Sikh Organisations UK. Alice Way, Hanworth Road, Hounslow, Middlesex, TW3 3VA.

Guru Gobind Singh Foundation, 1700 Pasture Brookway, Potomac, MD 20854 USA.

Guru Nanak (Sikh) Mission, 506 Aspen Dr., Lombard, IL 60148 USA.

Sikh Dharma International, 1620 Press Road, P.O. Box 351149, Los Angeles, CA 90035 USA.

Zoroastrians are followers of the teachings of Zarathushtra (known in Greek) as Zoroaster, who lived in North Eastern Iran, perhaps as long ago as 6,000 BCE or maybe nearer 1,200 BCE. Zarathushtra taught that Ahura Mazda, the Wise Lord, is the Supreme All-powerful God, who is a friend to all. Human beings are called to be fellow-workers with Ahura Mazda in ensuring the ultimate defeat of evil. The main Zoroastrian scripture is the Avesta, of which the Gathic Yasna, or Divine

Hymns of Zarathushtra, are especially important. There are only about 130,000 Zoroastrians alive today. The largest communities are in Iran and in Bombay, where they are known as Parsees.

World Zoroastrian Organisation, 135 Tennison Road, South Norwood, London SE25 5NF.

Zoroastrian Trust Funds of Europe (Inc), Zoroastrian House, 88 Compayne Gardens, West Hampstead, London NW6 3RU.

FEZANA, the Federation of Zoroastrian Associations of North America, 5750 S. Jackson St., Hinesdale, IL 60521 USA.

For information about interfaith work

Center for World Thanksgiving, Thanks-Giving Square, PO Box 1770, Dallas, TX 75221 USA

CoNexus Press, c/o Joel Beversluis, 6264 Grand River Drive, Ada, MI 49301 USA.

Council for a Parliament of the World's Religions, PO Box 1630, 105 W. Adams, Suite 800, Chicago, IL 60690-1630 USA.

International Association for Religious Freedom (IARF), 2 Market Street, Oxford OX1 3EF, UK; *and* 576 Fifth Avenue #1103, New York, NY 10036 USA.

International Interfaith Centre, 2 Market Street, Oxford OX1 3EF, UK.

Interfaith Center of New York, 570 Lexington Avenue at 51st St., 22nd Floor, New York NY 10022 USA.

Inter Faith Network for the UK, 5-7 Tavistock Place, London WC1H 9SS UK.

Inter Religious Federation for World Peace, 4 West, 43rd St. New York, NY 10036 USA.

Multifaith Resources, c/o Rev. Charles White, PO Box 128 Wofford Heights, CA 93285 USA.

North American Interfaith Network, c/o Dr. Peter Laurence, 512 Bedford Road, Armonk, NY 10504 USA.

Peace Council, Suite 108, Madison, W153704, USA.

The Shap Working Party in World Religions, c/o The National Society's RE Centre, 36 Causton Street, London SW1P 4AU.

World Conference on Religion and Peace (WCRP), WCRP/International, 777 UN Plaza, New York, NY 10017 USA

United Religions Initiative, PO Box 29242, Presidio Building #1009, 1st Floor, San Francisco, CA 94129-0242 USA.

World Congress of Faiths, 2 Market Street, Oxford OX1 3EF, UK.

Estimates of the number of adherents of various religions are only approximations.

BIBLIOGRAPHY

General

Armstrong, K., *Holy War,* Macmillan, 1988; Doubleday, 1991.

A Bibliographical Guide to the Comparative Study of Ethics, Eds. Carman, J. and Juergensmeyer, M., Cambridge University Press, 1991.

Chichester D., *Patterns of Action: Religion and Ethics in a Comparative Perspective,* Wadsworth, 1987.

Cohn-Sherbok, D., *World Religions and Human Liberation,* Orbis, 1991.

Cole, W. Owen, *Moral Issues in Six Religions,* Heinemann Educational, 1991.

Green, R.M., *Religion and Moral Reason,* Oxford University Press, 1988.

Making Moral Decisions, Eds. Holm, J with Bowker J., Pinter, 1994

Jenkins, J., *Contemporary Moral Issues,* Heinemann, 1993.

Women in World Religions Ed. Sharma A., SUNY, 1987.

World Religions

There are many introductory books about the religions of the world and their teachings on ethics, including:

Dictionary of Beliefs and Religions, Ed. Goring, Rosemary and Whaling, Frank, Chambers, 1992; Larousse, 1994.

Ethical Issues in Six Religious Traditions: Ed. Morgan, Peggy and Lawton, Clive, Edinburgh University Press, 1996; Columbia University Press, 1996.

Fisher, Mary Pat and Luyster, Robert, *Living Religions,* I.B. Tauris, 1990, and Revised 2nd Edtn 1996.

Neusner, J., *World Religions in America,* Westminster/John Knox, 1994.

Our Religions, Ed. Sharma A., HarperSanFrancisco, 1993.

The Oxford Dictionary of World Religions, Ed. Bowker, J., Oxford University Press, 1997.

Religions in the UK: A Multi-Faith Directory, Ed. Fry, Eileen and Weller, Paul, University of Derby, 1997.

Religious Traditions of the World, Ed. Earhart, Byron, HarperSanFrancisco, 1993.

Smart, Ninian, *The World's Religions,* Cambridge University Press, 2nd edtn 1998; Prentice Hall, 1989.

Smith, Huston, *The World's Religions,* HarperSanFrancisco, 1991.

A Source Book for Earth's Community of Religions, Ed. Beversluis, Joel, CoNexus Press, 1993 and 1995 Revised Edition.

The World's Religions: Understanding the Living Faiths, Ed. Clarke, Peter B., The Reader's Digest 1993.

World Scripture: A Comparative Anthology of Sacred Texts, Ed. Wilson, Andrew, Paragon House 1991.

Young, William A., *The World's Religions: Worldviews And Contemporary Issues,* Prentice Hall, 1995.

The Global Ethic

A Global Ethic: The Declaration of the Parliament of the World's Religions, Ed. Hans Küng and Karl-Josef Kuschel, SCM Press and Continuum, 1993.

A Global Ethic and Global Responsibilities, Ed. Hans Küng and Helmut Schmidt, SCM Press and Continuum, 1998.

Braybrooke, Marcus, *Stepping Stones to a Global Ethic,* SCM Press, 1992.

Küng, Hans, *Global Responsibility: In Search of a New World Ethic,* SCM Press and Continuum, 1991.

Küng, Hans, *A Global Ethic for Global Politics and Economics,* SCM Press, 1997.

Yes to a Global Ethic, Ed. Hans Küng, SCM Press and Continuum, 1996.

Explorations in Global Ethics, Eds. Sumner B. Twiss and Grelle, Bruce, Westview Press, 1998.

The Parliament of World Religions

Braybrooke, Marcus, *Pilgrimage of Hope: One Hundred Years of Global Interfaith Dialogue*, SCM Press and Crossroad, 1992.

Braybrooke, Marcus, *Faith and Interfaith in a Global Age*, CoNexus Press and Braybrooke Press, 1998.

The Community of Religions, Ed. Teasdale, Wayne and Cairns, George, Continuum, 1996.

The Dawn of Religious Pluralism: Voices from the World's Parliament of Religions, 1893, Ed. Seagar, Richard Hughes, Open Court, 1993.

Seagar, Richard Hughes, *The World's Parliament of Religions*, Indiana University Press, 1995.

Baha'i

'Abdu'l-Baha, *Faith For Everyman*, Baha'i Publishing Trust, London, 1972.

'Abdu'l-Baha, *Foundations of World Unity*, Baha'i Publishing Trust, Wilmette, 1945.

'Abdu'l-Baha, *Paris Talks* (11th ed), Baha'i Publishing Trust, 1969.

'Abdu'l-Baha, *Promulgation of Universal Peace*, Baha'i Publishing Trust, 1982.

'Abdu'l-Baha, *Some Answered Questions*, Baha'i Publishing Trust, n.d.

'Abdu'l-Baha, *Secret of Divine Civilization*, 2nd ed, Baha'i Publishing Trust, 1970.

'Abdu'l-Baha, *Selections from the Writings of 'Abdu'l-Baha*, Baha'i World Centre, Haifa, 1978.

Baha'i Prayers, National Spiritual Assembly, USA, 1954.

Baha'i Peace Program, Baha'i Publishing Committee, NY, 1930.

Baha'u'llah and 'Abdu'l-Baha, *Baha'i World Faith: Selected Writings of Baha'u'llah and 'Abdu'l-Baha*, Baha'i Publishing Trust, Wilmette, 1956.

Baha'u'llah, *Epistle to the Son of the Wolf*, Baha'i Publishing Trust, Wilmette, 1971.

Baha'u'llah, *Gleanings From the Writings of Baha'u'llah*, Baha'i Publishing Trust, 1952

Baha'u'llah, *Hidden Words*, Baha'i Publishing Trust, London, 1932.

Baha'u'llah, *The Kitab-i-Iqan: The Book of Certitude*, Baha'i Publishing Trust, 1961.

Baha'u'llah, *Tablets of Baha'u'llah*, Baha'i World Centre, 1978.

Brahma Kumaris

Living Values: A Guide Book, Brahma Kumaris World Spiritual University, 1995.

The Companion of God, The Wisdom and Words of Dadi Janki, Brahma Kumaris World Spiritual University, 1996.

Buddhism

Aitken, R., *The Mind of Clover*, North Point Press, 1985.

Buddhism and Ecology, Ed. Batchelor, M. and Brown, K., Cassell, 1992.

Dalai Lama, *Beyond Dogma, the challenge of the modern world*, Souvenir Press, 1994.

Gross, R., *Buddhism after Patriarchy*, SUNY, 1993.

Jayatilleke, K.N., *Ethics in a Buddhist Perspective*, Wheel Publications, n.d.

Jones, K., *Beyond Optimism: A Buddhist Political Ecology*, Jon Carpenter, 1994.

Jones, K., *The Social Face of Buddhism*, Wisdom Books, 1989.

Kapleau, P., *To Cherish all Life*, Buddhist Publishing Group, 1986.

Keown, D., *The Nature of Buddhist Ethics*, Macmillan, 1992; St Martin's Press, 1992.

Keown, D., *Buddhism and Bioethics*, Macmillan, 1995.

King, W., *In the Hope of Nibbana*, Open Court, 1964.

Misra, G.S.P., *Development of Buddhist Ethics*, Munshiram Manoharlal, 1984.

Saddhatissa, H., *Buddhist Ethics*, Allen & Unwin, 1970; G. Braziller, 1971.

Sangharakshita, *Buddhism, World Peace and Nuclear War*, Windhorse, 1984.

Sizemore, R.F., and Swearer, D.K., *Ethics, Wealth and Salvation*, South Carolina, 1990.

Stott, D., *A Circle of Protection for the Unborn*, Ganesha Press, 1986.

Tachibabam S., *The Ethics of Buddhism*, Curzon Press, 1992.

Thich Nhat Hanh, *Love in Action*, Parallax, 1993.

The Dharmapada (sayings of the Budda) – various publishers.

Walpola, Rahula, *What the Buddha Taught*, Oneworld Publications, 1996.

Also see World Wide Web sites 'Buddhism'. 'Engaged Buddhism'.

Christianity

(*Unless indicated otherwise the Biblical references are RSV*)

Arnold, J.C. *A Plea for Purity - Sex, Marriage and God*, Plough, 1996.

Brailsford, H.N. *The Levellers and the English Revolution*, Spokesman, 1976.

Christianity and Ecology, Ed. Breuilly, E. and Palmer, M., Cassell, 1992.

Brown, D., *Choices*, Basil Blackwell, 1983.

A New Dictionary of Christian Ethics, Ed Childress, J. and Macquarrie, J., SCM Press, 1987.

Ethical Dilemmas: Crises in Faith and Modern Medicine, Ed. Chirbban, J.T., University Press of America, 1994.

Ferguson, J. *The Politics of Love: The New Testament and Non-violent Revolution*, Sheldon Press 1977.

Froehlich, K., 'Inquisition' in Grolier Electronic Publishing, 1996.

Gill, R., *Christian Ethics in Secular Worlds*, T & T Clark, 1991.

Gutierrez, G. *Theology of Liberation*, Orbis, 1973.

Helwys, T. , *The Mistery of Inquity*, London, 1612.

Hutterian Brethen and Yoder, J.H. *God's Revolution - The Witness of Eberhard Arnold*, Paulist Press, 1984.

Linzey, A., *Animal Theology*, SCM Press, 1994.

Parry, Abbott and de Waal, E., *The Rule of St Benedict*, Gracewing, 1990.

Sider, R. , *Christ and Violence*, Lion, 1980; HeraldPress, 1979.

Wink, W., *Engaging the Powers - Discernment and Resistance in a World of Domination*, Fortress, 1992.

Yearly Meeting of the Religious Society of Friends, *Quaker Faith and Practice*, 1995.

Yoder, J.H., *When War is Unjust - Being Honest in Just War Thinking*, Orbis, 1996.

Hinduism

Akekar, A.S., *The Position of Women in Hindu Civilisation*, Motilal Banarsidass, 1962.

Doniger, W., *The Laws of Manusmriti*, Penguin, 1991.

Coward, H.G., Lipner J.J. and Young K.K., *Hindu Ethics*, SUNY, 1989.

Crawford, S.C., *The Evolution of Hindu Ethical Ideals*, University Press of Hawaii, 1982

Gandhi, M.K., *The Story of My Experiments with Truth*, Navajivan, 1927.

Jackson, R. and Killingley, D., *Moral Issues in the Hindu Tradition*, Trentham, 1991.

Jhingran, S., *Aspects of Hindu Morality*, Motilal Banarsidass, 1989.

Roles and Rituals for Hindu Women, Ed. Leslie, J., Pinter, 1991.

Mahadevan, T.M.P., *Outlines of Hinduism*, Chetana, 2nd edtn 1960.

Prime, R., *Hinduism and Ecology*, Cassell, 1992.

Hinduism Today (International Newspaper), 107 Kaholalele Road, Kapaa. HI 96746 USA.

Islam

Al Faruqi, Ismail R., *Islam*, Argus Communications, 1979.

'Ali', A.Y. (trans.), *The Holy Qur'an*, Islamic Foundation, 1995. (The Arabic text with English translation).

Bowker, John, *Voices of Islam,* Oneworld Publications, 1995.

Esposito, J.L., *Islam - The Straight Path*, Oxford University Press, 1994.

Fakhry, M., *Ethical Theories in Islam*, E. J. Brill, Leiden, 1991.

Haddad, Y.Y. and Lummis, A.T., *Islamic Values in the United States*, Oxford University Press, 1987.

al-Kaysi, M.I., *Morals and Manners in Islam*, Islamic Foundation, 1984.

Khalid, F.M., and O'Brian, J., *Islam and Ecology*, Cassells, 1992.

Memissi, F., *Women and Islam*, Oxford, 1987.

Rahman, F., *Health and Medicine in the Islamic Tradition,* The Crossroad Publishing Co., 1987.

Padwick, Constance, *Muslim Devotions*, Oneworld Publications, 2nd edtn, 1996.

Jainism

Bhargava, D., *Jain Ethics* Motilal Banarsidass, Delhi, 1968.

Bhattacharyya, N., *Jain Philosophy: Historical Outline*, Munshiram Manohalal, New Delhi, 1976.

Dundas, P., *The Jains*, Routledge, London, 1992.

Jain, J. P., *Religion and Culture of the Jains*, Bharatiya Jnanpith, New Delhi, 1975.

Jaini, P. S., *The Jaina Path of Purification*, University of California Press, Berkeley, 1979.

Jaini, P. S., *Gender and Salvation: Jaina Debates on the Spiritual Liberation of Women*, University of California Press, Berkeley, California, 1991.

Laidlow, J., *Riches and Renunciation: Religion, Economy and Society among the Jains*, Clarendon Press, Oxford, 1995.

Marett, P., *Jainism Explained,* Jain Samaj Europe Publications, Leicester, 1985.

Nahar, P. C., and Ghosh, J. C., *Encyclopedia of Jainism*, Sri Satguru Publications, Delhi, 1986.

Sogani, K. C., *Ethical Doctrines in Jainism*, Jaina Samskrita Samrakshaka Sangha, Sholapur, 1967.

Judaism

Biale, R., *Women and Jewish Law*, Schocken, 1984.

Breslauer, S.D., *Contemporary Jewish Ethics: A Bibliographical Survey*, Greenwood, 1985.

Buber, M., *I and Thou*, T. & T. Clark 1958; Scribner, 1958

Danby, H.H., *The Mishnah,* Oxford University Press, 1933.

Contemporary Jewish Ethics and Morality: A Reader, Ed. Dorff, E.N. and Newman, E., Oxford University Press, 1995

Herring, B.F., *Jewish Ethics and Halakhah for Our Time,* Ktav, 1984.

Jacobvits, I., *Jewish Medical Ethics*, rev.edn, Bloch, 1975.

Jacobs, L., *Jewish Personal and Social Ethics*, Behrman, 1990.

Landau, R.S. , *The Nazi Holocaust*, London: I.B. Tauris, 1992; I. R. Dee, 1994.

Rose, A., *Judaism and Ecology*, Cassell, 1992.

Solomon, N., *Judaism and World Religion,* Macmillan, 1991; St Martin's Press, 1991.

Hebrew Bible.

Midrash Rabbah, Soncino Press.

Babylonian Talmud, Soncino Press.

Forms of Prayer for Jewish Worship, Reform Synagogues of Great Britain.

Rastafarian

Amen, I, R.U.N: Metu Neter, Vol.1: *The great Oracle of Tehuti and the Egyptian system of spiritual cultivation*, Khemit Corp., 1990.

Barrett, Leonard E. : *The Rastafarians: The Dreadlocks of Jamaica*, Heinemann, 1977; Beacon Press 1977.

Bhavnani, K.K. and Coulson, M. 'Transforming socialist feminism: The Challenge of racism'. in *Feminist Review*, Vol.23, 1986.

Brah, A., 'Women of South Asian origin in Britain', In *South Asian Research,* vol.7(1), 1987.

Brah, A., 'Difference, diversity and differentiation', in James Donald and Ali Rattansi Ed., *'Race'. Culture and Difference,* Sage Publications, 1993.

Brah, A., and Minhas, R., 'Structural racism or cultural difference: Schooling for Asian girls' in Weiner, G., Ed., *Just a bunch of girls,* Open University Press, 1985.

Carby, H., : 'White women listen! Black feminism and the boundaries of sisterhood.' In CCCS: *The Empire Strikes back,* Hutchinson, 1982.

Chevannes, Barry. Rastafari: *Roots and Ideology,* Syracuse University Press, 1994.

Davis, Angela, Y. *Women, culture and politics,* Vintage Books, 1990

Garvey, Marcus, *Philosophy and Opinions of Marcus Garvey,* Ed., Garvey, Amy Jacques, Antheneum, 1992.

Knowles, Caroline and Mercer, Sharmila 'Feminism and anti-racism: An exploration of the political possibilities' In James Donald and Ali Rattansi, Ed., *'Race', Culture and Difference,* 1993.

Sikhism

Alag, Sarup Singh, *Excellence of Sikhism,* published by the author, Ludhiana, 1996.

Cole, W. Owen, *The Sikhs, Their Religious Beliefs and Practices,* Routledge and Kegan Paul, 1978.

Cole, W.O. and Sambhi, P.S., *The Sikhs: Their Religious Beliefs and Practices,* Sussex Academic Press, 1995.

Kaur, K. and Singh I., (trans.), *Rehat Maryādā: A Guide to the Sikh Way of Life,* 1971.

Kohli, Surinder Singh, *Sikh Ethics,* Munshiram Manohar Lal Publishers Pvt Ltd., 1975.

Dogra and Mansukhani, *Encyclopaedia of Sikh Religion and Culture,* Vikas Publishing House, 1996.

Mansukhani, Gobind Singh, *Aspects of Sikhism,* Punjabi Writers' Cooperative Society Ltd, 1982.

Sharomani Gurdwara Parbandhak Committee, Sikh Rehat Maryada: *A Guide to the Sikh Way of Life,* Amritsar, 1978.

Singh, Harbans, *The Message of Sikhism,* Delhi Sikh Gurdwara Management Committee, 1978.

Singh, Harbans, *Encyclopaedia of Sikhism,* Punjabi University, 1995.

Singh, Manmohan, *Sri Guru Granth Sahib translation* (CGS), Shiromani Gurdwara Parbandhak Committee, 1981.

Unesco, *The Sacred Writings of the Sikhs,* George Allen & Unwin Ltd, London, 1973.

Singh, A., *Ethics of the Sikhs,* Punjabi University, 1983.

Singh, N., *The Sikh Moral Tradition: Ethical Perception of the Sikhs in the Late Nineteenth and Early Twentieth Centuries,* Manohar, 1990.

In addition, original and secondary sources in Panjabi have been used. Translations from Guru Granth Sahib have been done by the contributor.

Zoroastrianism

Boyce, Mary, *History of the Zoroastrianism: Their Religious Beliefs and Practices,* Mary Boyce, Routledge & Kegan Paul, 1979.

Firby, Nora K., *European Travellers and their Perceptions of the Zoroastrians in the 17th & 18th Centuries,* Dietrich Reimer, 1988, Berlin.

Frye, Richard N., *The Golden Age of Persia,* Weidenfeld & Nicholson, (1975) 1988.

Hinnell, John R., *Zoroastrianism and the Parsis Ward,* Lock International, 1981.

Mehr, Farhang, *The Zoroastrian Tradition,* Element, 1991.

William, Jackson, A. V., *Zoroaster, the Prophet of Ancient Iran,* Columbia University Press (Macmillan), New York, 1899, 1965.

There are various translations of the Gathas, for example by Insler, 1975 and Davond, P.

Fezana Journal, published quarterly by the Federation of Zoroastrian Associations of North America, 5750 S. Jackson St., Hinesdale, IL 60521 USA.

A Non-Religious Viewpoint

Dover, N., 'World Poverty', in *A Companion to Ethics*, Ed. Singer P., Blackwell, 1993.

Hardin, G., 'Lifeboat Ethics', in *World Hunger and Moral Obligation*, Ed. Aitken W. and La Foliette, H., Prentice Hall, 1977.

Kant, I., *Lectures on Ethics* , Methuen, 1963; Cambridge University Press, 1997.

Singer, P., *Famine, Affluence and Morality in Philosophy and Public Affairs,* Vol 1,3, 1972.

Singer, P. *Practical Ethics,* Cambridge University Press, 2nd Edtn 1993.

LIST OF CONTRIBUTORS

Charanjit Ajitsingh, (Sikh). Lecturer and writer on Sikhism. She has been involved in developing interfaith relations at all levels. She has recently retired from her position as Assistant Director of Schools from a Local Authority in London. (All Sikh contributions).

Mavis Badawi, (Muslim). Educational Psychologist, who works with young people. She is married to Dr Zaki Badawi, who is Principal of the Muslim College, London and a founder of the Three Faiths Forum. (All Muslim contributions).

Martine Batchelor, (Buddhist). Writer and teacher at Sharpham College of Buddhist Study and Contemporary Enquiry. She teaches meditation retreats world-wide. (Buddhist contributions to B; C1; D).

Shahin Bekhradnia, (Zoroastrian). Teacher on ancient history, classical civilisation and religious education. A speaker and writer on Zoroastrianism and Honorary Secretary of the World Congress of Faiths. (All Zoroastrian contributions).

Andrew Bolton, (Christian). Peace and Justice Co-ordinator of the Reorganised Church of Jesus Christ of Latter Day Saints. Formerly lecturer at Westminster College, Oxford and Religious Education Adviser, City of Leicester. (All Christian contributions).

Marcus Braybrooke, Parish priest, lecturer and writer on interfaith relations. Joint President, World Congress of Faiths and Trustee of the International Interfaith Centre, the Peace Council and the Council for a Parliament of the World Religions. (A1).

Bronwyn Elsmore, (Baha'i). Senior Lecturer in Religious Studies, Faculty of Humanities, Massey University, Palmerston North, New Zealand. (All Baha'i contributions).

S L Gandhi, (Jain). Hon. Secretary General of Anuvrat Global Organisation (ANUVIBHA) and International Advisor to the Intercultural Open University of Opeinde in the Netherlands. Author of several books on religious and ecological subjects. (Jain contribution to C1)

Arthur Dion Hanna, jr (AKA Ras Boom Skak) is a Rastafarian from the Bahamas, where he practised as an attorney for 15 years. He is now a doctoral student at the School of Oriental and African Studies (SOAS). Actively involved in human rights and civil liberty issues, he is a member of the Bahamas Law Guild, the National Conference of Black Lawyers of the USA and the Society of Black Lawyers of the UK. (All Rastafarian contributions).

Clive Lawton, (Jewish). Jewish educationalist and author. Former appointments include Education Officer for the Board of Deputies; Headmaster of King David's High School, Liverpool; Deputy Director for the Liverpool Education Authority; Chair of the Shap Working Party on World Religions in Education; and Director of Jewish Continuity. Co-editor of *Ethical Issues in Six Religious Traditions*. (Jewish contributions to C3; C4).

Sister Maureen, (Brahma Kumari). Programme Co-ordinator at the Brahma Kumaris International Centre in London, responsible for the University's outreach work in the UK in prisons, healthcare, education, women's issues, interfaith dialogue and other areas of community life. She is the Brahma Kumaris' representative to the United Nations in Vienna. (All Brahma Kumari contributions).

Werner Menski, (Hindu). Senior Lecturer in South Asian Law at the School of Oriental and African Studies at the University of London. He has contributed to many books on Hindu law, Indian marriage and matters relating to ethnic minorities in Britain. (All Hindu contributions).

Rachel Montagu, (Jewish). Educated at Newnham College, Cambridge; Leo Baeck College, London and Machon Pardes, Jerusalem. She teaches Judaism and Biblical Hebrew at Birkbeck College. (Jewish contributions to B; C1; C2; D).

Peggy Morgan, Senior Lecturer in Theology and Religious Studies, Westminster College, Oxford; Director, Religious Experience Research Centre, Oxford; Hon. Secretary, British Association for the Study of Religions; Trustee, International Interfaith Centre, Oxford. Author of several books on Buddhism and Co-editor of *Ethical Issues in Six Religious Traditions*. (A2).

John Newson (Buddhist). A Buddhist practitioner who is involved in social and community action in Birmingham, England. He is a follower of the Vietnamese Zen Master Thich Nhat Hanh and also a member of the UK Network of Engaged Buddhists. (Buddhist contributions to C2; C3; C4).

Glynn Phillips, (Non-religious worldview). A philosopher, presently lecturing in Philosophy at Nene University College, Northampton. His main interests are moral philosophy and philosophy of education and his main areas of publication are moral education and political education. (E)

INDEX OF RELIGIONS

CoNexus Press is a publisher and supplier of books on religious, interfaith, spiritual and global questions, including *A Sourcebook for Earth's Community of Religions.*

6264 Grand River Drive, Ada MI 49301, USA
Tel 616 682 9022. Fax 616 682 9023. E-mail conexus@iserv.net.

International Interfaith Centre is a registered charity, established by the International Association for Religious Freedom, Westminster College, Oxford and the World Congress of Faiths, for education and research into world-wide interfaith activity and as a support network for those engaged in this work. It arranges conferences and lectures, publishes a newsletter and offers advice and information on inter-faith activity.

2 Market Street, Oxford, OX1 3EF, UK.
Tel 01865 202745 fax 01865 202746 E-mail iic@interfaith-center.org.

World Congress of Faiths, a religious and educational charity, is a fellowship of individuals who seek to encourage understanding and co-operation between members of world religions. It arranges conferences, lectures and tours and publishes the journal *Word Faiths Encounter* and newsletter *One Family* and has produced *All in Good Faith*, a resource book for multi-faith prayer.

2 Market Street, Oxford, OX1 3EF, UK.
Tel 01865 202751 fax 01865 202746